HAPPY, HAPPY BIRTHDAY #9 EDDIE!
WE LOVE YOU SO MUCH!
MiMi + GG

# SCIENCE
# AND SPACE

9.3.18

HAPPY HAPPY BIRTHDAY 4 EDIE ♥
WE LOVE YOU SO MUCH! ♥
♥ ♥ ♥
MiMi + GG

An Hachette UK Company
www.hachette.co.uk

First published in Great Britain in 2017 by Bounty Books,
a division of Octopus Publishing Group Ltd
Carmelite House, 50 Victoria Embankment
London EC4Y 0DZ
www.octopusbooks.co.uk

Copyright © Octopus Publishing Group Ltd 2017

Edited and designed by Anna Bowles and Perfect Bound Ltd

ISBN 978 0 7537 3238 0

Printed and bound in China

1 3 5 7 9 10 8 6 4 2

Publisher: Lucy Pessell
Designer: Lisa Layton
Editor: Natalie Bradley
Proofreader: Jane Birch
Administrative Assistant: Sarah Vaughan
Production Controller: Sarah Kulasek-Boyd

Artworks created by Perfect Bound Ltd

# COLOR + LEARN
# SCIENCE AND SPACE

## MORE THAN 200 PAGES OF FASCINATING FACTS + COLORING

Bounty
Books

# CONTENTS

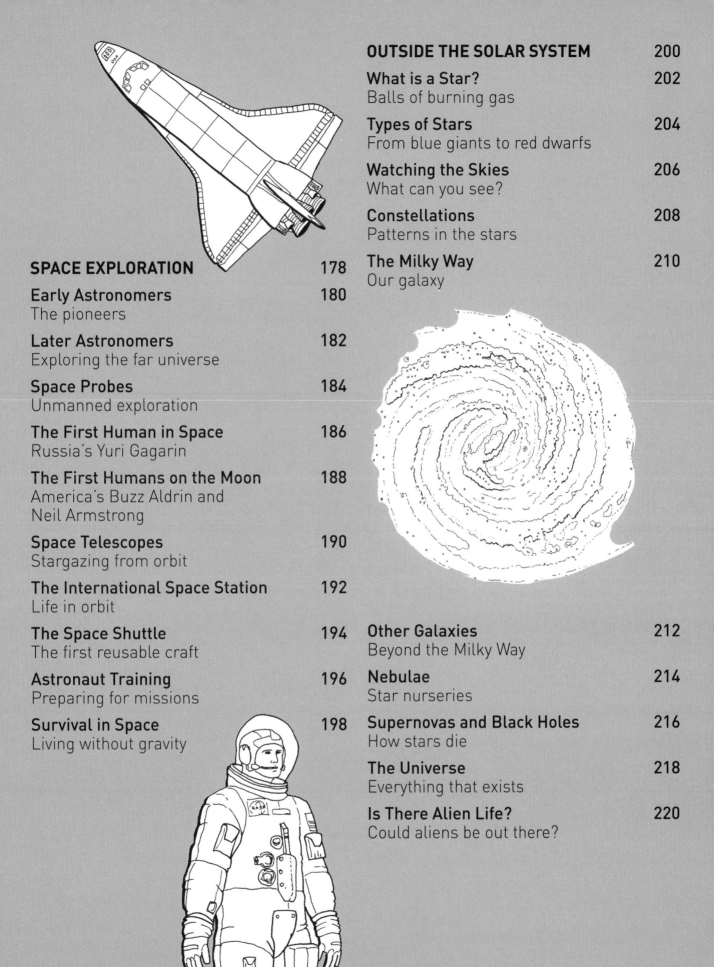

# SCIENCE AND SPACE

Science tells us how our world works. Everything that exists has to follow one set of natural laws that shape reality. Understanding science helps humans to create inventions that transform our lives and make Earth a better place... or to fly beyond it, and explore outer space!

## QUICK FACTS

**CHOCOLATE** was invented 1,000 years ago.

There are billions of **STARS** in the Universe.

Earth's **CRUST** is made up of 30 separate plates.

A **TSUNAMI** can move at up to 600 miles per hour.

Sometimes the water in a river can flow **BACKWARD**.

Antarctica is the world's largest **DESERT**.

The tropical **RAINFORESTS** are thought to contain thousands of species humanity has not discovered yet.

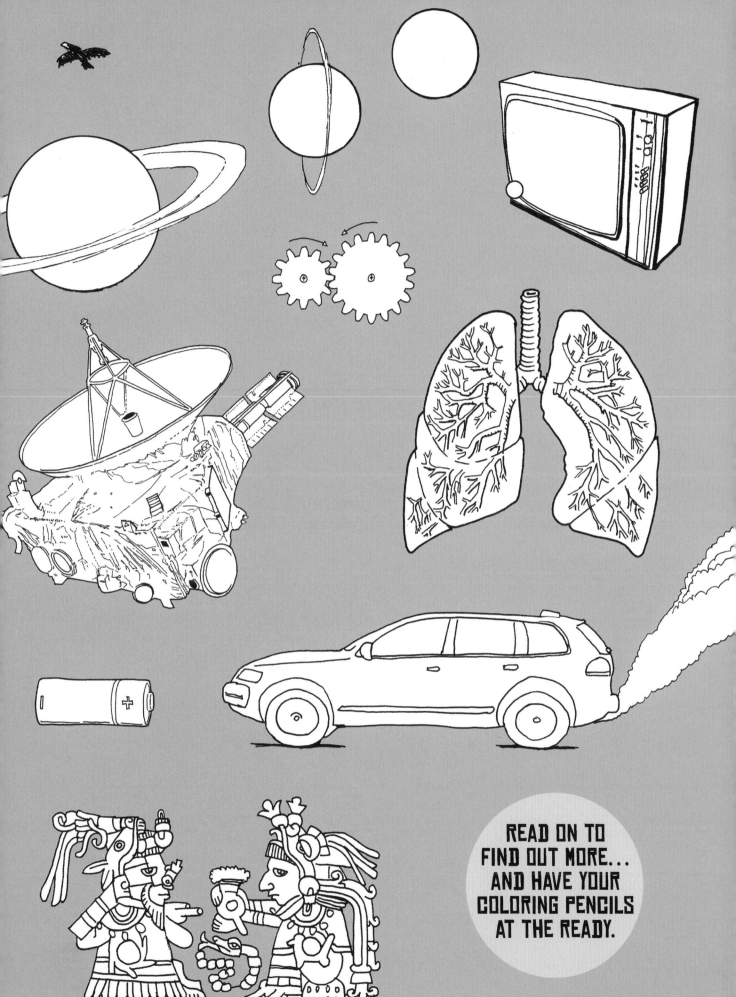

READ ON TO
FIND OUT MORE...
AND HAVE YOUR
COLORING PENCILS
AT THE READY.

# OUR WORLD

# THE EARTH

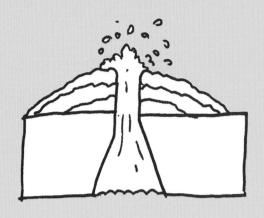

# VOLCANOES

When rock melts in the heat deep under Earth's surface, it expands and needs a lot more space. The pressure is so great under some areas that melted rock pools in cracks in the ground. When the pressure becomes greater than the roof of rock over it, it bursts out as a volcano.

During the eruption, hot gaseous liquid, or solid material, is blown out. The material piles up around the opening and a cone-shaped mound is formed.

## QUICK FACTS

The word **DORMANT** means "sleeping". So when people talk about a volcano being dormant, it means it is temporarily sleeping and might erupt in the future.

In the year 79 CE, Mount Vesuvius, a volcano in Italy, violently erupted. The ash **BURIED** two nearby towns.

The world's largest **INACTIVE** volcano is in Hawaii, USA. It is called Haleakala, and rises to a height of about 10,025 ft.

In February 1943, in a cornfield in Mexico, people saw a volcano being **BORN**! In three months it had formed a cone about 1,000 ft high.

In 2010, a volcano in Iceland **ERUPTED**. The ash cloud disrupted air travel around the globe for several weeks.

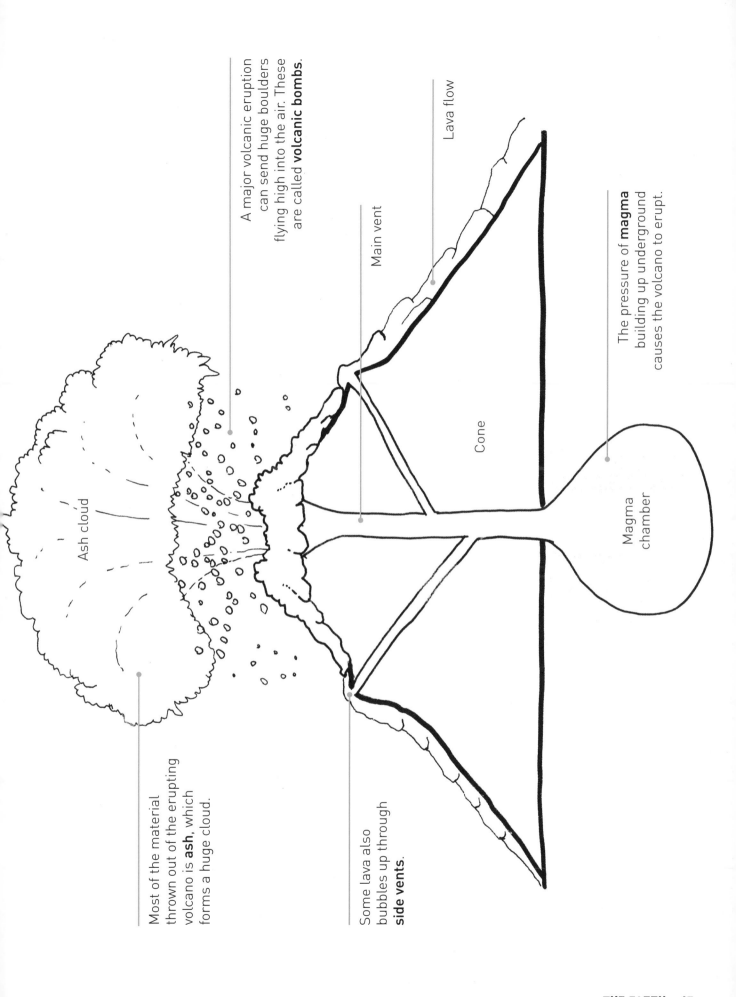

A major volcanic eruption can send huge boulders flying high into the air. These are called **volcanic bombs**.

Lava flow

Main vent

The pressure of **magma** building up underground causes the volcano to erupt.

Cone

Magma chamber

Ash cloud

Most of the material thrown out of the erupting volcano is **ash**, which forms a huge cloud.

Some lava also bubbles up through **side vents**.

# THE EARTH'S CRUST

The crust is made of three types of rock: sedimentary, igneous, and metamorphic.

Of these, the sedimentary rocks are formed from fragments that are laid down as layers, or beds. Igneous rocks are formed when molten material from inside Earth cools and solidifies. Metamorphic rocks are the result of already existing rocks being heated and compressed by Earth's movements to such an extent that their minerals change.

## QUICK FACTS

The **INSIDE** of Earth is divided into three parts: the mantle, the outer core, and the inner core.

Usually the **MINERALS** that make up rock form distinct crystals. It is easy to see the crystals in some rocks.

Earth's **CRUST** is moving all the time, and sometimes land is pushed into huge folds—mountains.

**BASALT** is a very fine-grained rock that comes from volcanoes.

Many sedimentary rocks contain shells, bones, and other remains of living things. These are called **FOSSILS**.

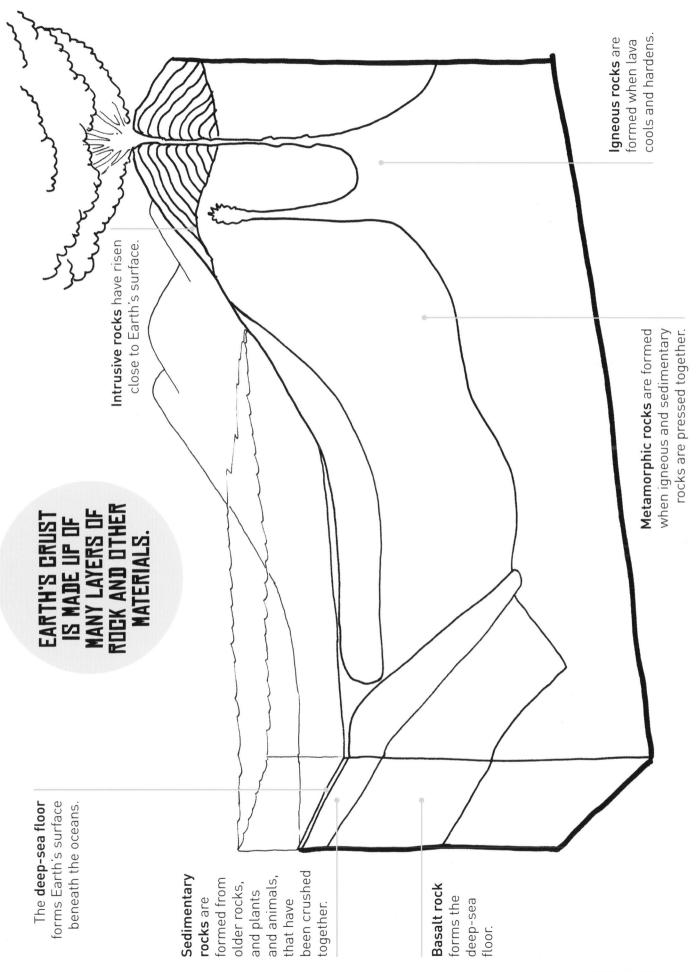

**Igneous rocks** are formed when lava cools and hardens.

**Intrusive rocks** have risen close to Earth's surface.

**Metamorphic rocks** are formed when igneous and sedimentary rocks are pressed together.

EARTH'S CRUST IS MADE UP OF MANY LAYERS OF ROCK AND OTHER MATERIALS.

The **deep-sea floor** forms Earth's surface beneath the oceans.

**Sedimentary rocks** are formed from older rocks, and plants and animals, that have been crushed together.

**Basalt rock** forms the deep-sea floor.

# MOUNTAINS

Mountains are formed as the result of violent changes in Earth's surface, most of which happened millions of years ago.

Most mountains are formed when Earth's tectonic plates move. As layers of rocks push against each other, they buckle and fold at the edges. Mountains are pushed up at upfolds, and valleys are formed in downfolds.

## QUICK FACTS

Some mountain **PEAKS** stand alone, but most mountains are joined together to form a range.

**MOUNT EVEREST**, which is in the Himalayas, is 29,030 ft high. Humans first reached the summit in 1953.

The **HIMALAYAS** is a vast mountain range formed by the crumpling of Earth's surface as India moves northward and collides with Asia.

The **APENNINE** mountains stretch almost the entire length of Italy.

**ROCKSLIDES** are common where forests have been destroyed on mountainsides. There are no longer any tree roots to stabilize the loose material.

**Folded** mountains are made of rock layers that have been squeezed by great pressure into large folds.

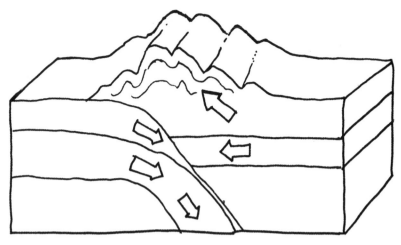

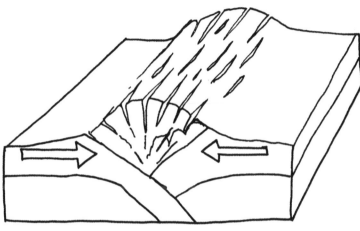

In **dome** mountains, the rock layers are forced up to make greater blister-like domes on the surface of Earth.

**Volcanic** mountains are made up of lava, ash, and cinders which poured out from Earth's core.

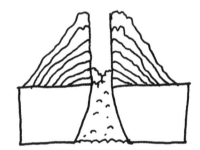

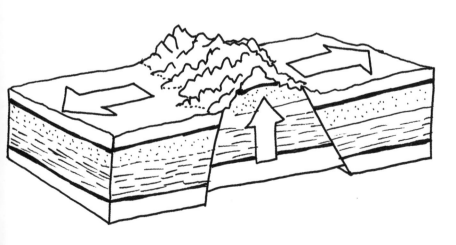

**Block** mountains are the result of breaks, or faults, in Earth's crust.

# EARTHQUAKES

Every 30 seconds on our planet, the ground rumbles and trembles. Most of the movements are so slight that they are not felt. Others can be so large they cause complete disaster. Big cracks appear in the land, streets buckle, and buildings simply crumble.

These are called earthquakes, and the reason they occur is because Earth's crust is made up of moving parts called tectonic plates. When these plates slide past or into each other, the rocks jolt and send out shock waves.

## QUICK FACTS

**MINING** and **TUNNELING** have caused earthquakes in areas that are already under tension due to movements in Earth's crust.

A **SEISMOGRAPH** picks up the vibrations of rocks rubbing together. It is used for predicting earthquakes.

Probably the best-known gauge of earthquake intensity is the **RICHTER** magnitude scale.

Earth's **CRUST** is made up of about 30 plates.

Most of the areas where earthquakes take place are along the **EDGES** of these plates.

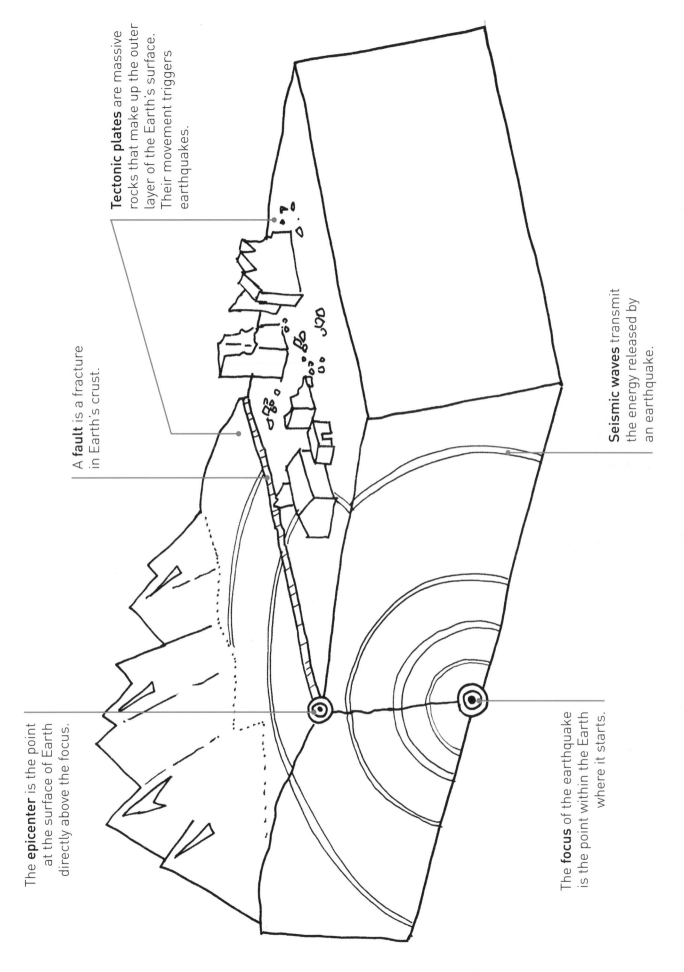

**Tectonic plates** are massive rocks that make up the outer layer of the Earth's surface. Their movement triggers earthquakes.

A **fault** is a fracture in Earth's crust.

**Seismic waves** transmit the energy released by an earthquake.

The **epicenter** is the point at the surface of Earth directly above the focus.

The **focus** of the earthquake is the point within the Earth where it starts.

# EROSION

Erosion is a natural process by which rock and soil are broken loose from Earth's surface at one location and moved to another.

It begins with a natural effect called weathering. Environmental factors break rock and soil into smaller pieces and loosen them from Earth's surface.

## QUICK FACTS

Erosion changes land by wearing down **HILLS**, filling in **VALLEYS**, and causing rivers to appear and disappear.

A chief cause of erosion is the formation of ice. As water **FREEZES**, it expands. When it freezes inside the crack of a rock, it can break the rock apart.

The power of erosion by **GLACIERS**, snow, and rivers is huge. Over millions of years they grind down mountains.

Erosion can be speeded up by such human activities as **FARMING** and **MINING**.

One of the most harmful effects of erosion is that it robs farmland of productive **TOPSOIL**.

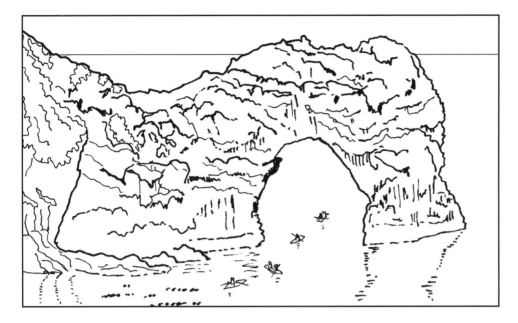

Erosion by **waves** creates amazing rock formations like Durdle Door in Somerset, England.

Wind and sand erode the **rock** into fascinating shapes in the deserts of North America.

**Rivers** gradually erode their banks.

# RIVERS

Rivers are formed very slowly, as excess rain and melted snow or ice from glaciers makes its way from the land to the sea.

Water drains through the ground into small streams, which join up with others as they flow downhill, eventually forming a river in the bottom of a valley.

## QUICK FACTS

At 4,132 miles long, the **NILE** is Earth's longest river.

The farther a river is from its **SOURCE** on a mountainside, the slower the water travels. This is because the river eventually reaches flatter ground.

Usually water flows **DOWN** a river, but near the coast the flow is reversed as the tide comes in.

Sometimes the flow reverses **NATURALLY**. This is called a tidal bore.

Tidal bores happen in the Amazon in South America, where there is a bore as high as **15 FT**.

A smaller **BORE** travels up the River Severn in England.

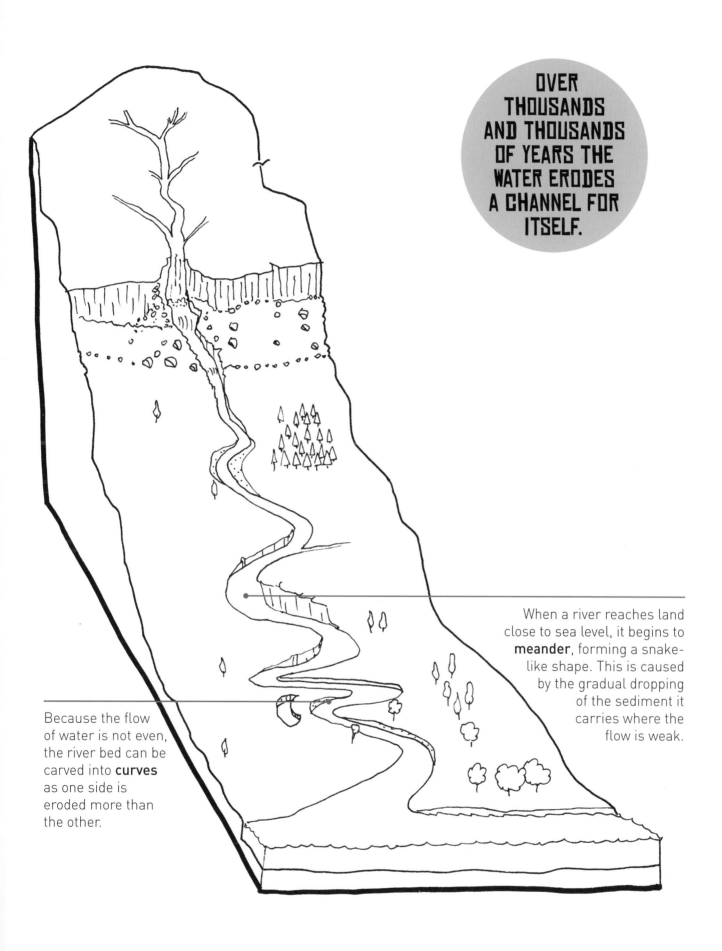

When a river reaches land close to sea level, it begins to **meander**, forming a snake-like shape. This is caused by the gradual dropping of the sediment it carries where the flow is weak.

Because the flow of water is not even, the river bed can be carved into **curves** as one side is eroded more than the other.

# GLACIERS

Glaciers are large massses of ice that form on land and move slowly under their own weight. They begin to take shape when more snow falls during the winter than melts and evaporates in summer. The excess snow gradually builds up in layers, and its increasing weight causes the snow crystals under the surface to become compact. The ice eventually becomes so thick that it moves under the pressure of its own great weight.

## QUICK FACTS

Glaciers have shaped most of the world's highest **MOUNTAINS**, carving out huge **VALLEYS**.

**LAKES** are formed from flooded glacial valleys that become dammed by debris as the glacier melts.

At the height of the **ICE AGE**, ice sheets reached as far south as the River Thames in southern England.

High in the Alps, Pyrenees, and other mountains, glaciers remain, though many are **SHRINKING**.

Some scientists think that we are currently undergoing an "**INTERGLACIAL**"—a period of warming during a longer Ice Age—and that the ice may one day advance again.

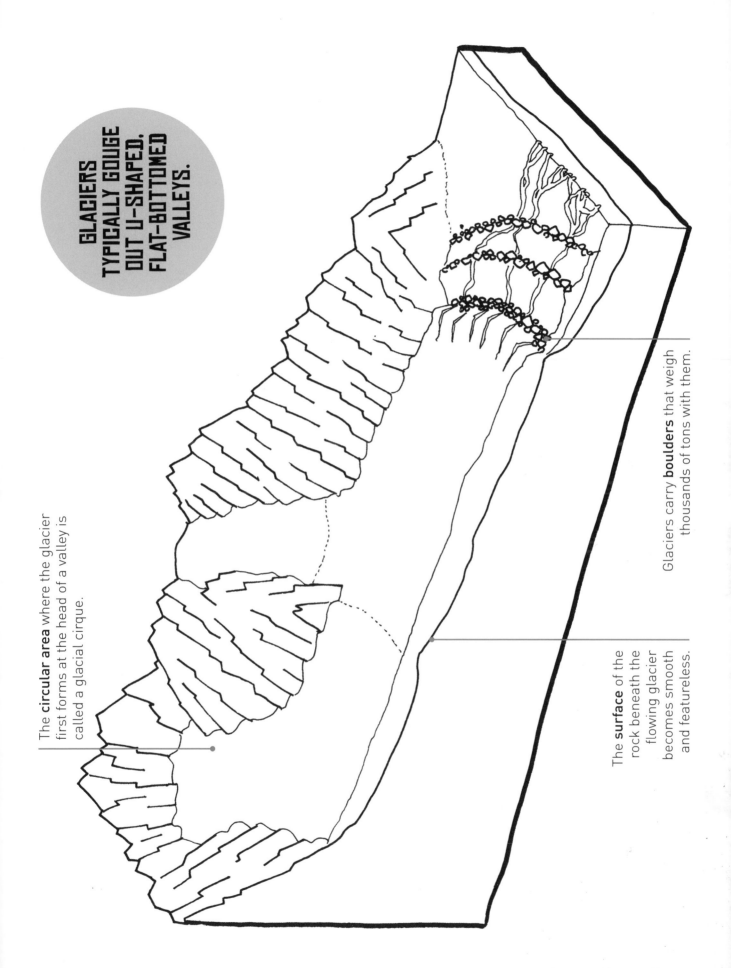

**GLACIERS TYPICALLY GOUGE OUT U-SHAPED, FLAT-BOTTOMED VALLEYS.**

The **circular area** where the glacier first forms at the head of a valley is called a glacial cirque.

Glaciers carry **boulders** that weigh thousands of tons with them.

The **surface** of the rock beneath the flowing glacier becomes smooth and featureless.

# DESERTS

About one-third of the world's land surface is covered by desert. Deserts are found wherever there is too little water to allow much plant life to grow. Salt deserts form when shallow seas and lakes dry up, leaving a deposit of smooth salt.

## QUICK FACTS

The world's largest hot desert is the **SAHARA** in northern Africa. It stretches from the Atlantic Ocean in the west to the Red Sea in the east.

The Sahara has about 90 large oases, where there is enough water for people grow **CROPS**.

**MIRAGES** form in deserts where the air is so hot it bends and distorts light rays. The shimmering images that a mirage produces often trick travellers.

The **HOTTEST** shade temperature was in Libya in 1922, when the temperature in the Sahara reached 136.5°F.

Because a desert is defined by the amount of rainfall or snowfall it receives, the **LARGEST** desert in the world is in fact the icy continent of Antarctica.

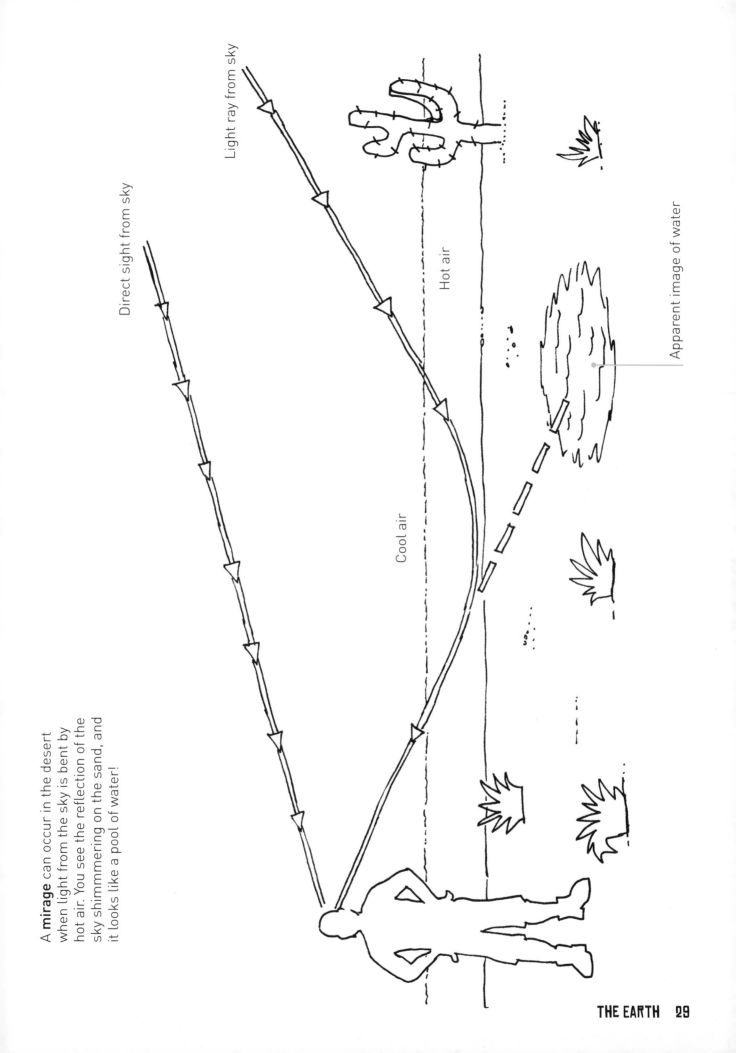

A **mirage** can occur in the desert when light from the sky is bent by hot air. You see the reflection of the sky shimmmering on the sand, and it looks like a pool of water!

Light ray from sky

Direct sight from sky

Hot air

Cool air

Apparent image of water

# OCEANS

Oceans cover most of the Earth. The Pacific alone forms more than one-third of the surface, and contains more than half our world's water. Coastlines are constantly changing: either being eroded or built up.

The water is moved by the wind, and by movements within the ocean. These currents are able to transfer a great amount of heat around Earth as they move, and thus play a part in climate control.

## QUICK FACTS

The deepest places on Earth are **TRENCHES** in the oceans. Many trenches occur in the Pacific Ocean.

Scientists have since discovered a great variety of **LIVING THINGS** in the deep sea.

Waves arise from a combination of the wind and the shape of the **SEABED**. The wind blows the surface layers of the sea, gradually forming a rolling movement of the water.

The Pacific Ocean contains more than 30,000 **ISLANDS**.

All Earth's water is known as the **HYDROSPHERE**.

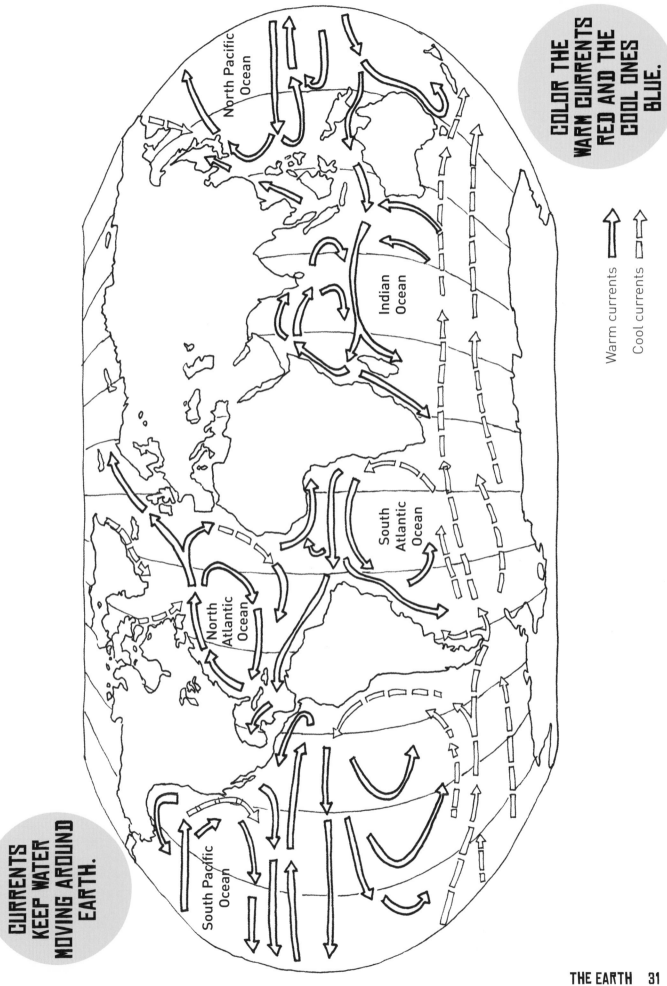

CURRENTS KEEP WATER MOVING AROUND EARTH.

COLOR THE WARM CURRENTS RED AND THE COOL ONES BLUE.

Warm currents

Cool currents

North Pacific Ocean

Indian Ocean

South Atlantic Ocean

North Atlantic Ocean

South Pacific Ocean

# TSUNAMIS

Tsunamis are large, destructive waves caused by earthquakes on the ocean floor. When an earthquake happens, it gives a tremendous push to the surrounding seawater, and this creates the waves.

Tsunamis may build to heights of more than 100 ft when they reach shallow water near shore.

## QUICK FACTS

Tsunamis can travel great distances while diminishing little in size, and can **FLOOD** coastal areas thousands of miles from their source.

In the open ocean, they typically move at **SPEEDS** of 500–600 miles per hour.

Another form of tsunami is called a **STORM SURGE**. This is caused when a violent storm whips up huge waves.

In 2004, the **INDIAN OCEAN** tsunami killed hundreds of thousands of people and destroyed the coastline.

Other dangerous water phenomena include **WHIRLPOOLS** and **ICEBERGS**.

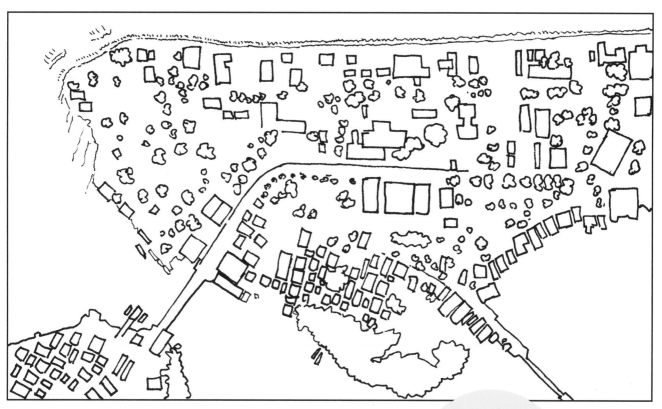

This area was a **town** before the tsunami washed over it.

THE INDIAN OCEAN TSUNAMI DEVASTATED ENTIRE TOWNS.

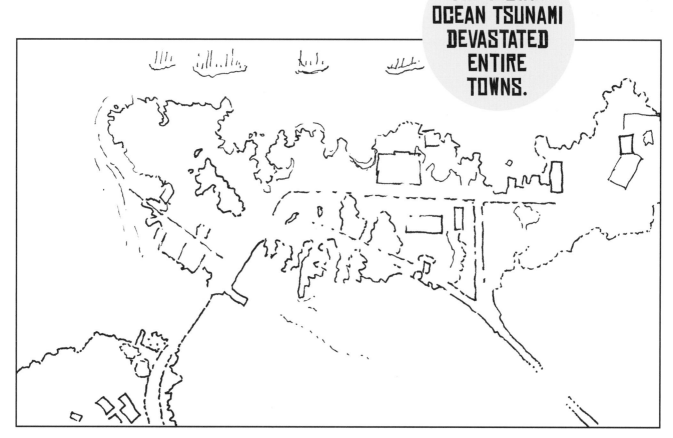

Almost all the buildings have been destroyed, and some areas that were previously land are now **under water** for good.

# RAINFORESTS

Rainforests are tropical evergreen forests. The climate is warm and moist all year round and offers an extraordinarily wide range of habitats for living things.

Quite apart from the fact that the canopy is vital to wildlife, the planet's trees are essential to us if we wish to survive. They produce fruit to feed a huge number of animals and their prey all year round.

## QUICK FACTS

Rainforests benefit people in **FOUR** major ways. They provide (1) economic, (2) scientific, (3) environmental, and (4) recreational value.

Tropical rainforests contain the most **VARIED** mixtures of animals and plants of any habitat on Earth.

It is estimated that over two million different **SPECIES** of plant and animal thrive in the rainforests.

Many of these species are **UNDISCOVERED** by humans.

Each year new rainforest plants are discovered, and valuable plant chemicals that can be used to treat human **DISEASES** are found.

THE AMAZON RAINFOREST IS AN AMAZINGLY RICH ENVIRONMENT.

Scientists divide the rainforest into five **layers** to study it.

Overstory

Canopy

Understory

Shrub layer

Forest floor

# DEFORESTATION

Deforestation has occurred on a huge scale in the past two decades. Humans are clearing the land to exploit it for growing food and new biofuel crops, and to provide tropical hardwood for construction.

Essentially, it is commercial greed that threatens this extraordinary habitat.

## QUICK FACTS

In 1950, rainforests covered about **8,700,000** square miles. This area would cover about three-quarters of Africa.

Today, less than **HALF** the original extent of Earth's rainforest remains.

Commercial logging, agriculture, mining, and hydroelectric dams have all **DAMAGED** or **WIPED OUT** extensive areas of rainforest.

Many areas of tropical rainforest are **BURNED**. The result after one or two years is useless, **INFERTILE** land that is prone to flash floods.

The destruction of Indonesian rainforests has left nowhere for the **ORANGUTAN** to live.

**HUMANS ARE DELIBERATELY BURNING THE RAINFOREST.**

Rainforest animals flee to the surviving trees. Most of them will **perish** when large areas of forest are cleared.

Once the fire is out, the land will be used for **farming** and **grazing** cattle.

# SEVEN NATURAL WONDERS OF THE WORLD

Although there is no official list, the following are generally accepted as the Seven Natural Wonders of the World.

## QUICK FACTS

**USA:** The huge Barringer Crater is a circular depression in the Earth.

**USA:** The Grand Canyon is a breathtaking 280-mile chasm created by the Colorado River eroding the rock.

**ASIA:** Mount Everest rises 29,030 ft above sea level in the Himalayas.

**EUROPE:** The Matterhorn, on the Italian-Swiss border, is one of the most beautiful mountains on Earth.

**AFRICA:** The spectacular Victoria Falls is on the Zambezi River between Zimbabwe and Zambia.

**AUSTRALIA:** The Great Barrier Reef is the world's longest coral reef formation.

**AUSTRALIA:** Uluru (Ayers Rock) rises 1,141 ft above the desert floor.

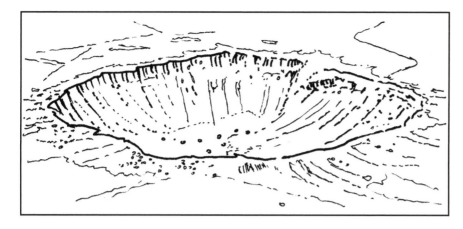

**Barringer Crater** was created by a meteorite impact.

The Colorado River has been carving the **Grand Canyon** for six million years.

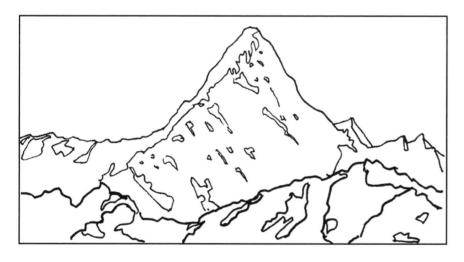

**Everest** is the world's highest mountain.

**Uluru** is a sacred site for local native Australians.

# THE WEATHER

# CLIMATE

Climate is the word we use to describe the seasonal pattern of hot and cold, wet and dry weather, averaged over 30 years.

As different parts of Earth are closer to the Sun for longer, the climate varies in different countries. Those nearest the equator are the hottest. Those nearest the poles are the coldest.

## QUICK FACTS

Winds and **OCEAN CURRENTS** distribute heat around the Earth.

The weather pattern in different regions will also be altered by the changing **SEASONS**, and some areas routinely have a higher level of annual rainfall than others, while some countries remain very dry.

Mountains, such as the Rockies in North America, have a typical **ALPINE** climate because of their height.

Over millions of years the human body has altered to suit the climates of different regions. In general, the hotter the region, the **DARKER** the skin of its inhabitants.

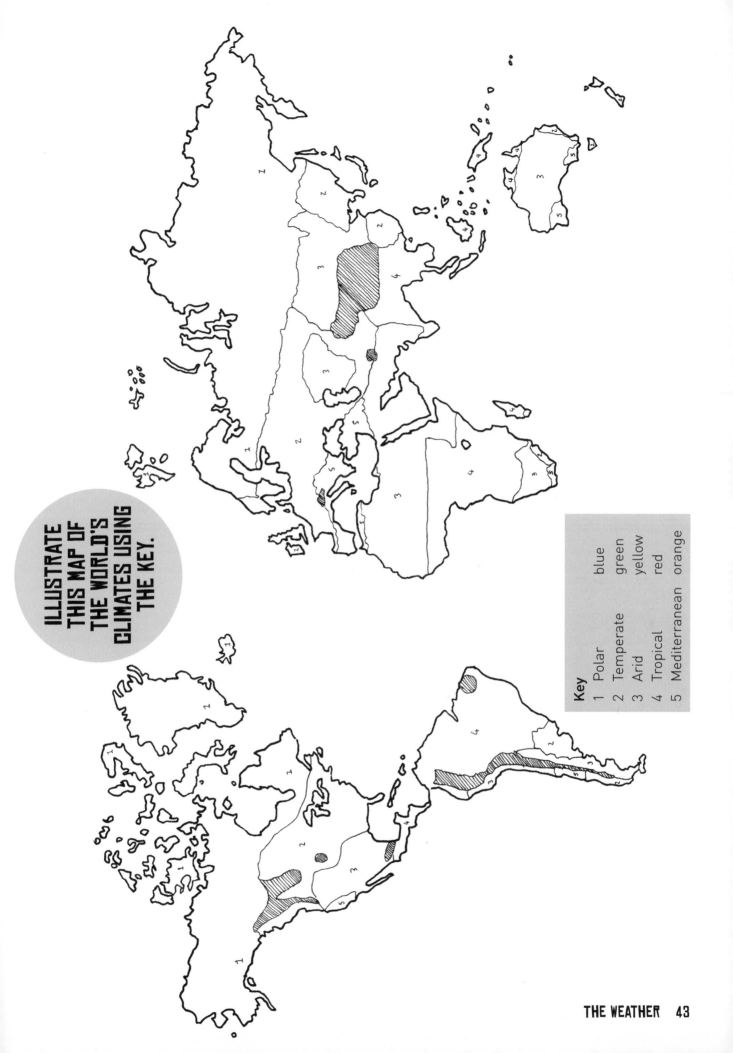

ILLUSTRATE THIS MAP OF THE WORLD'S CLIMATES USING THE KEY.

**Key**
1 Polar          blue
2 Temperate      green
3 Arid           yellow
4 Tropical       red
5 Mediterranean  orange

# THE SEASONS

We have seasons because Earth is tilted on its axis. As Earth moves round the Sun, the hemisphere tilted toward the Sun receives more sunlight, and this is summer time. The days are longer and the weather is warmer because of the extra amount of sunlight. The hemisphere tilted away from the Sun receives less sunshine, has shorter days, and is cooler. This is winter time.

## QUICK FACTS

**HEMISPHERE** is the name given to any half of the globe. It comes from a Greek word that means "half a sphere".

The **EQUATOR** is an imaginary line drawn around the outside of the Earth. It divides the Earth into two halves.

The area near to the equator is always exposed to the Sun's rays, so it is **WARM** all the year round.

The equator was invented by **MAPMAKERS**. It makes a convenient point from which to measure distances.

In the northern hemisphere, the shortest day of the year is in the **WINTER SOLSTICE**, which is December 21, and the longest day is June 21, which is the **SUMMER SOLSTICE**.

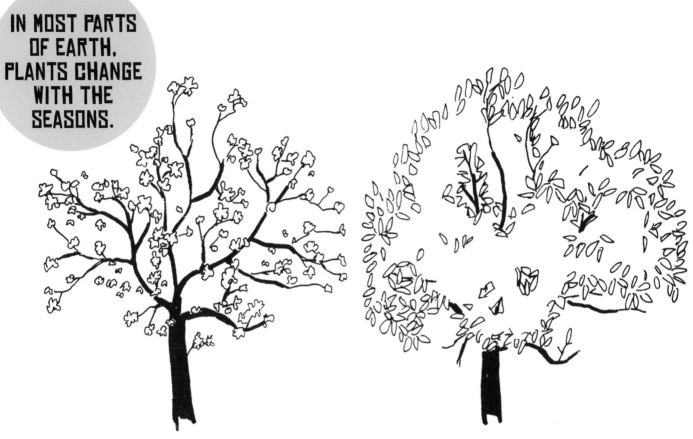

IN MOST PARTS OF EARTH, PLANTS CHANGE WITH THE SEASONS.

Deciduous trees bud in the **spring**.

They bear fruit in **summer**.

They lose their leaves in **fall (autumn)**.

They are bare during the **winter**.

# THE WATER CYCLE

People use billions of gallons of fresh water every day.

In nature, water circulates through a system called the water cycle. This cycle begins when heat from the Sun causes ocean water to evaporate. The vaporized water in the atmosphere gradually cools and forms clouds. The water eventually falls as rain or snow. Most falls into the oceans, but some falls on the land and flows back to the seas, completing the cycle.

## QUICK FACTS

In some areas of the world where there is no **RAIN** for long periods of time, local water cycles stop.

There are two main sources of **FRESH** water: surface water and ground water.

**SURFACE** water flows over the land in lakes, rivers, and streams.

**GROUND** water seeps through the soil or through tiny cracks in rock.

Too much rainwater can cause damage on the land. Flooding washes away fertile soil, and begins **ERODING** the ground.

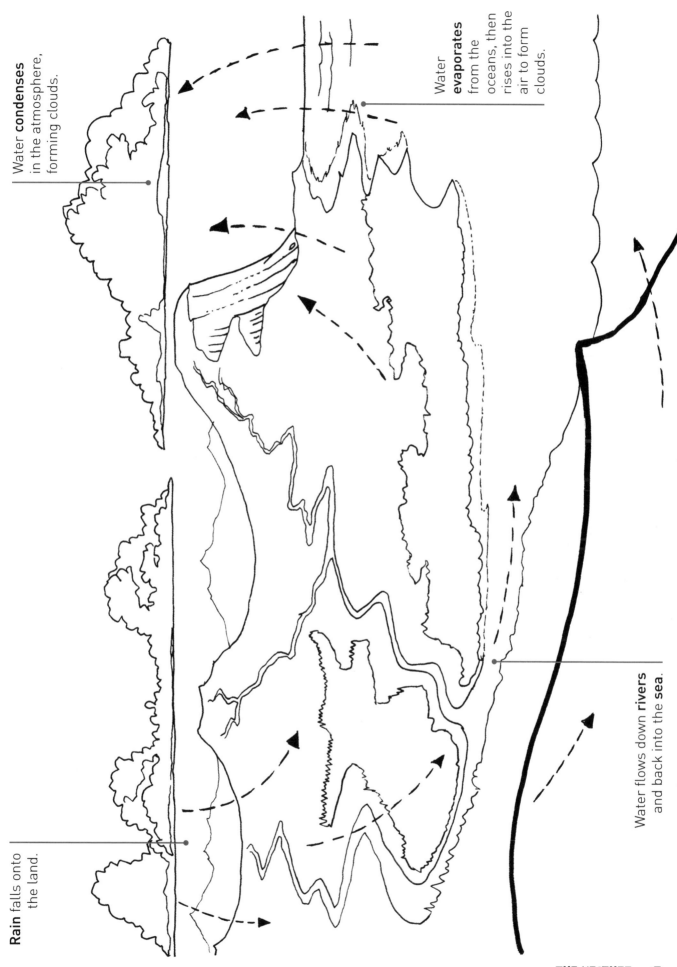

Water **condenses** in the atmosphere, forming clouds.

Water **evaporates** from the oceans, then rises into the air to form clouds.

**Rain** falls onto the land.

Water flows down **rivers** and back into the **sea.**

# RAIN

There is always water vapor in the air. It only takes a small drop in temperature to make the vapor condense and form tiny droplets of water.

If the air is very moist, the droplets cannot evaporate. Instead, they get bigger and bigger as more and more condensation takes place. Soon, each tiny droplet has become a drop. The drops start to fall downward, and we have rain.

## QUICK FACTS

A **RAINBOW** is a band of colors caused by the breaking up of light which has passed through raindrops.

The rain that falls is known as **PRECIPITATION**.

Different kinds of **CLOUD** form at different heights because of the differences in temperature.

Very high clouds are formed of **ICE CRYSTALS**.

**ACID RAIN** is a term for rain, snow, sleet, or other wet precipitation that is polluted by such acids as sulphuric acid and nitric acid.

Acid rain harms thousands of lakes, rivers, and streams worldwide, **KILLING** fish and other wildlife.

Drizzle

Downpour

Deluge

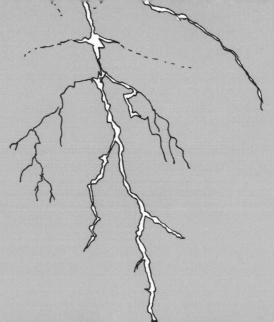

# STORMS AND LIGHTNING

Lightning is actually electricity. A huge electrical charge can be built up in certain weather conditions, and this leads to thunderstorms when a bolt of lightning leaps between the Earth and a cloud. The air is heated to a tremendous temperature, causing the explosive noise of thunder as it suddenly expands.

Lightning can kill you, so stay indoors during storms!

## QUICK FACTS

A lightning strike discharges about 100 million **VOLTS** of electricity.

Lightning **HEATS** the air in its path to more than 59,432°F.

Lightning **STRIKES** at 186,300 miles per second.

A lightning **CONDUCTOR** is a metal rod pointing upward from the highest point of a tall building. If lightning strikes, it hits the conductor, not the building.

Benjamin Franklin (1706–1790) discovered the nature of lightning while flying a **KITE** in a thunderstorm. He saw sparks jumping from a key tied to the end of the wet string.

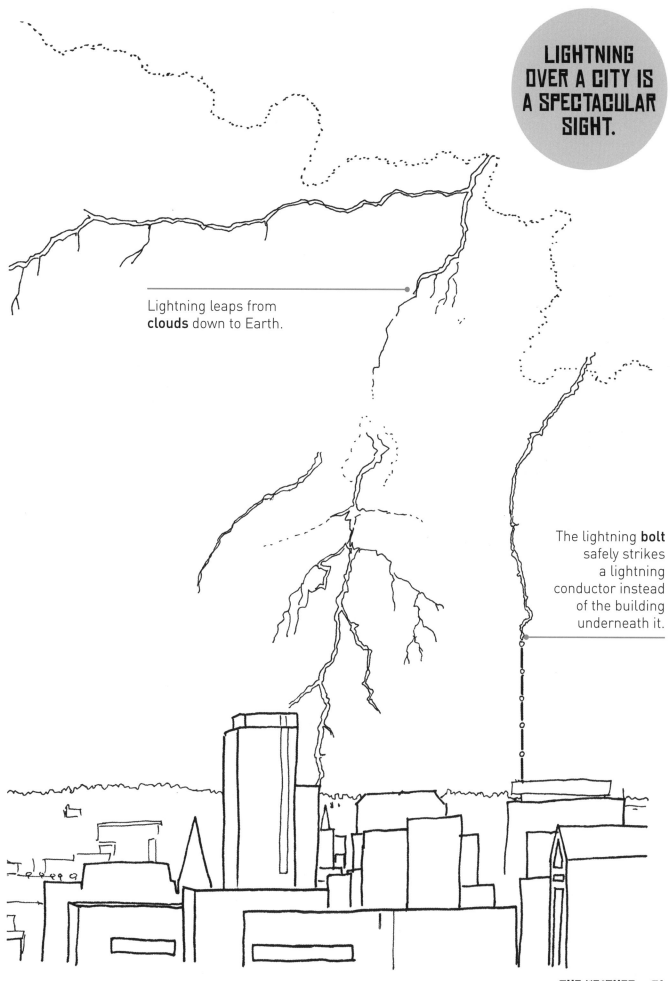

Lightning leaps from **clouds** down to Earth.

The lightning **bolt** safely strikes a lightning conductor instead of the building underneath it.

# FLOODS AND DROUGHTS

Flooding occurs when water cannot drain away fast enough via rivers. In areas of non-porous rocks, water runs off the land very quickly, and streams and rivers soon overflow.

Drought is a condition that results when the average rainfall for an area drops far below the normal amount for a long period of time. In areas that are not irrigated (artificially supplied with water), the lack of rain causes farm crops to wither and die.

## QUICK FACTS

Floods can also occur inland, when heavy rain drains off the land and causes rivers to **BURST** their banks.

Flooding also happens when winter snows **THAW** in spring.

This effect is made worse in **BUILT-UP** areas where the rain cannot soak into the ground.

Many **CITIES**, such as Venice in Italy and Bangkok in Thailand, are low lying and threatened by flooding.

Higher than normal **TEMPERATURES** usually accompany periods of drought. These high temperatures increase the stresses on plants and add to the crop damage.

Flooding **destroys** buildings, as well as drowning people.

During droughts, people have to seek water from **wells** deep underground.

# HURRICANES

Hurricanes are caused by storms. They draw large amounts of heat and moisture from the sea.

By the time a storm reaches hurricane intensity, it usually has a well-developed "eye" at its middle. Surface pressure drops to its lowest in the eye. In the eye of the storm, warm air spirals upward, creating the hurricane's strongest winds. The speed of the winds in the eyewall is related to the diameter of the eye.

## QUICK FACTS

A storm achieves hurricane status when its winds exceed **74 MILES PER HOUR**.

The **PEAK** time for hurricanes that affect the Gulf of Mexico and the west of the North Atlantic Ocean is from August to September.

Elsewhere, such storms are called **TYPHOONS** and tropical **CYCLONES**.

Approximately **85** hurricanes, typhoons, and tropical cyclones occur in a year throughout the world.

The end of a hurricane comes quickly if it moves over **LAND**, because it no longer receives heat energy and moisture from warm tropical water.

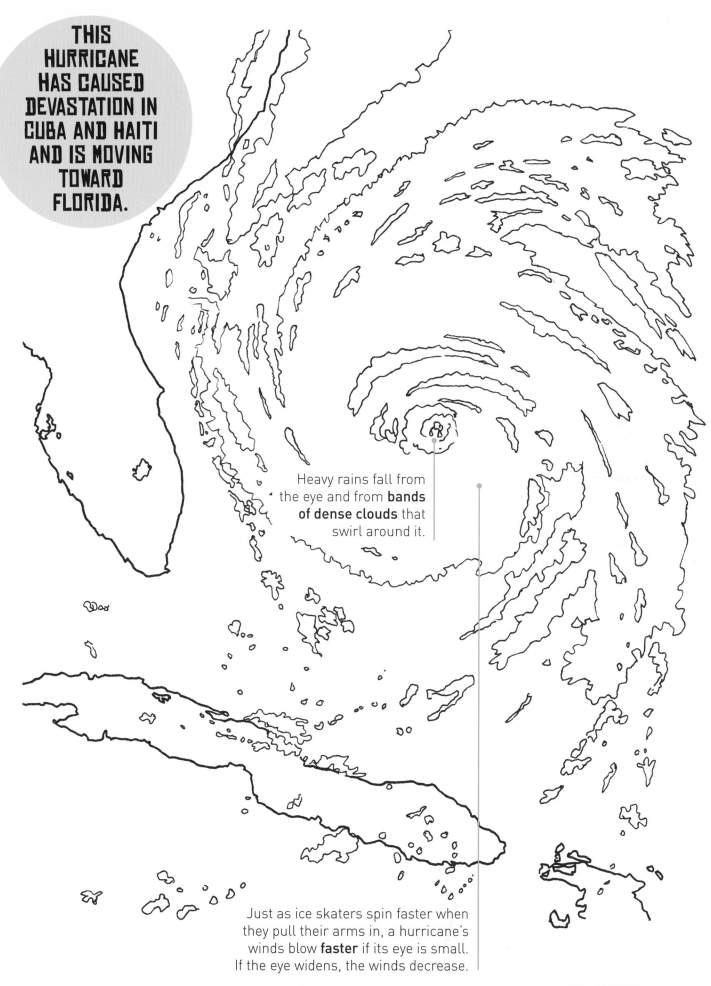

THIS HURRICANE HAS CAUSED DEVASTATION IN CUBA AND HAITI AND IS MOVING TOWARD FLORIDA.

Heavy rains fall from the eye and from **bands of dense clouds** that swirl around it.

Just as ice skaters spin faster when they pull their arms in, a hurricane's winds blow **faster** if its eye is small. If the eye widens, the winds decrease.

# FOG AND MIST

Tiny water droplets condensing from moist air cause fog and mist to arise. The water droplets can occur at ground level. The air can only hold a limited amount of water; if it suddenly cools, its capacity to hold water is reduced, which results in a mist or fog.

When fog occurs, visibility can be affected quite badly. Mist is less dense, however.

## QUICK FACTS

Mist commonly occurs on **CALM**, **CLEAR** nights, when heat rises, forming a thin layer of mist near the ground.

Mist often forms **OVER WATER**, because a mass of warm air passes over a cold stretch of water.

Fog **PARTICLES** are tiny. When you have a dense fog and can't see in front of you, it is because there may be as many as 20,000 of these particles in 1 cubic inch.

Over land, mist and fog often appears in enclosed **VALLEYS**, where cooling air flows gently down the sides of the hills to condense lower down.

Sometimes visibility is affected in built-up areas due to mist and fog, and can be mistaken for **SMOG**. Smog is a build up of exhaust fumes and factory smoke.

The top of the **hill** remains completely uncovered.

The mist is **thinner** the higher you go, so you can see the trees through the top layer.

Mist often forms low down in **valleys**, so that tall trees poke out of it.

# ENERGY

# LIGHT

Light is a form of energy that travels in waves through the air. It moves faster than anything else in the Universe.

We think of ordinary light as being "white", but really light is a mixture of red, orange, yellow, green, blue, and violet. When sunlight strikes a soap bubble, for example, it is broken up into the different wave lengths that are seen by our eyes. This band is called a "spectrum".

## QUICK FACTS

Lasers are beams of light that can **CUT** metal.

In **DVD PLAYERS** laser light scans the DVD's silvery surface, reading the tiny changes in light reflected back.

**MIRRORS** are pieces of glass that have been coated with a reflective material on the back, so that when a beam of light strikes the surface none of it is absorbed.

As light is split by water droplets into a **RAINBOW**, colors are always produced in the same sequence: red, orange, yellow, green, blue, indigo, and violet.

# THE SPEED OF LIGHT

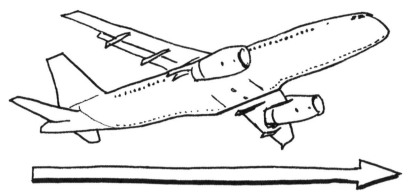

A **jet plane** would take about 20 years to reach the Sun.

**Car**: about 170 years.

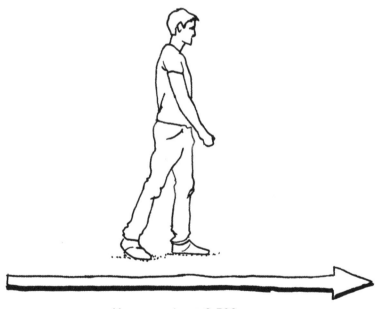

**Human**: about 3,500 years.

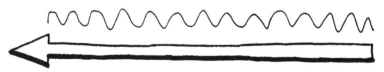

**Light**: about 8 minutes.

**HOW FAST IS LIGHT? IT'S AMAZINGLY FAST!**

# SOUND

Sounds travel as waves, and it is the shape of the sound wave that determines the kind of sound that will be produced. The pitch of the sound (whether high or low) depends on the frequency (rate of vibration) of the sound waves.

Musical instruments produce sounds in various different ways, but they all cause air to vibrate, which is how it carries the sound to your ears.

## QUICK FACTS

If a plane flies fast enough, it will go faster than sound waves. This is called breaking the **SOUND BARRIER**.

Sound waves travel through water. Ships can work out what is on the seabed by transmitting sound waves downward. This is called **SONAR.**

Sonar is used by **FISHERMEN** to detect shoals of fish.

It can also be used to detect submarines or to find **WRECKS** on the seafloor.

**BATS** use sonar to find their way around.

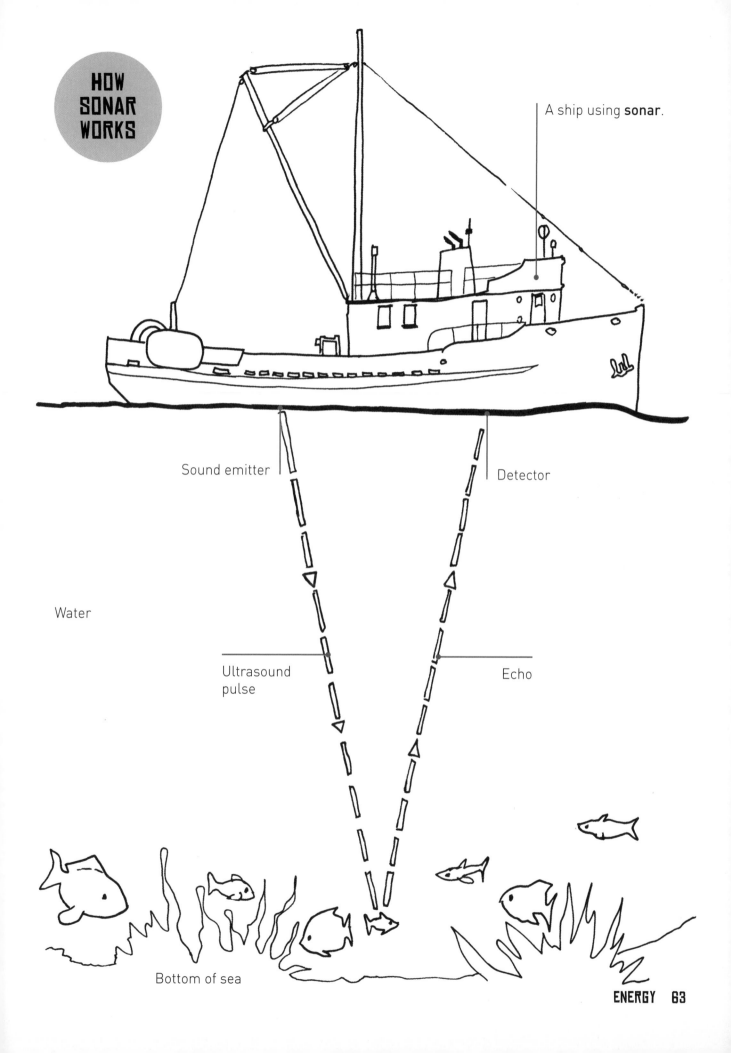

**HOW SONAR WORKS**

A ship using **sonar**.

Sound emitter

Detector

Water

Ultrasound pulse

Echo

Bottom of sea

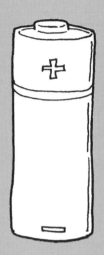

# ELECTRICITY

Electricity is used as a way of moving energy from place to place. Most powered devices in the home contain an electric motor.

When an electric current passes along a wire near a magnet, it exerts a force to move the wire. Usually the magnet is still, while the coil carrying the current spins around inside it.

## QUICK FACTS

Electric current can be produced by **BATTERY** cells.

In an electric **LIGHT BULB**, a current is passed through a filament of metal. It becomes white hot and gives us light.

**PYLONS** are connected by powerful electrical cables. Energy travels down these cables at about 250,000 kilometres a second.

Electric **CARS** have been in use for many years.

**WHEELCHAIRS** powered by electric batteries enable disabled people to move as fast as pedestrians.

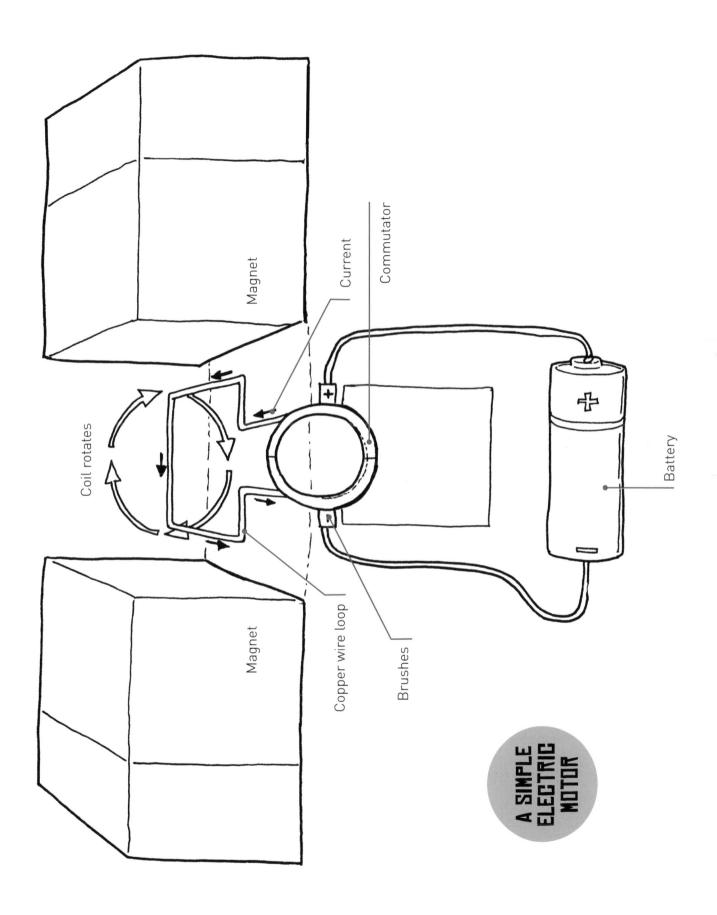

Magnet

Current

Commutator

Coil rotates

Magnet

Copper wire loop

Brushes

Battery

A SIMPLE ELECTRIC MOTOR

# FOSSIL FUELS

Fossil fuels, which include oil, coal, and natural gas, were formed millions of years ago when prehistoric plants and animals died. Their decaying bodies were pressed under layers of rock and earth, and became fossilized.

Not only are fossil fuels burned to supply heat and energy to our homes and industry, but by forming the fuel for power stations, they also supply most of the electricity we use.

## QUICK FACTS

Fossil fuels can be processed to produce many other useful materials, including **PLASTICS** and dyes.

The carbon and hydrogen in **OIL** can be made to join up in different ways to make more than 500,000 products.

One product is **GASOLINE [PETROL]**, which is the most common fuel used to power our cars.

Geologists know what kinds of rocks are likely to contain or cover oil **DEPOSITS**. When they find a likely area on land or at sea, test drilling is carried out.

**COAL** formed from the remains of tree ferns during the Carboniferous period, 359–299 million years ago.

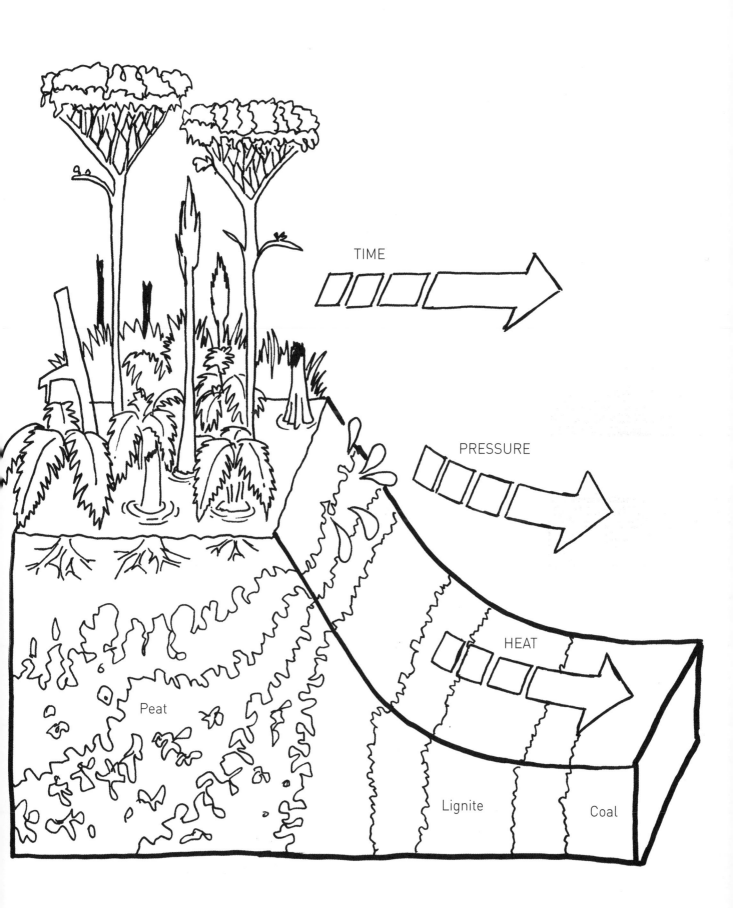

TIME

PRESSURE

HEAT

Peat

Lignite

Coal

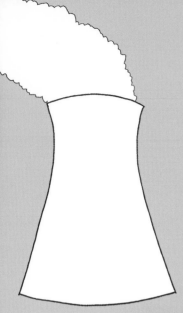

# NUCLEAR ENERGY

Inside a nuclear power station, billions of uranium atoms are torn apart, creating an enormous amount of energy. The energy is powerful enough to boil water, and steam from this hot water is used to generate electricity.

An atom is the tiniest unit of matter. The splitting of the atom was first observed under laboratory conditions in the late 1930s. It releases huge amounts of energy.

## QUICK FACTS

Nuclear energy could provide **CHEAP** and **UNLIMITED** power, but there are safety concerns.

When the energy is released from an atom, deadly rays called **RADIATION** can escape.

The nuclear reactor at a power station is surrounded by thick concrete walls for **SAFETY**.

In 1986, an explosion occurred at the **CHERNOBYL** nuclear power station in Ukraine. Contaminated clouds carried radiation across the world.

Nuclear **WEAPONS** were first used in 1945, at the end of World War II. Two bombs were dropped on the Japanese cities of Hiroshima and Nagasaki by the US.

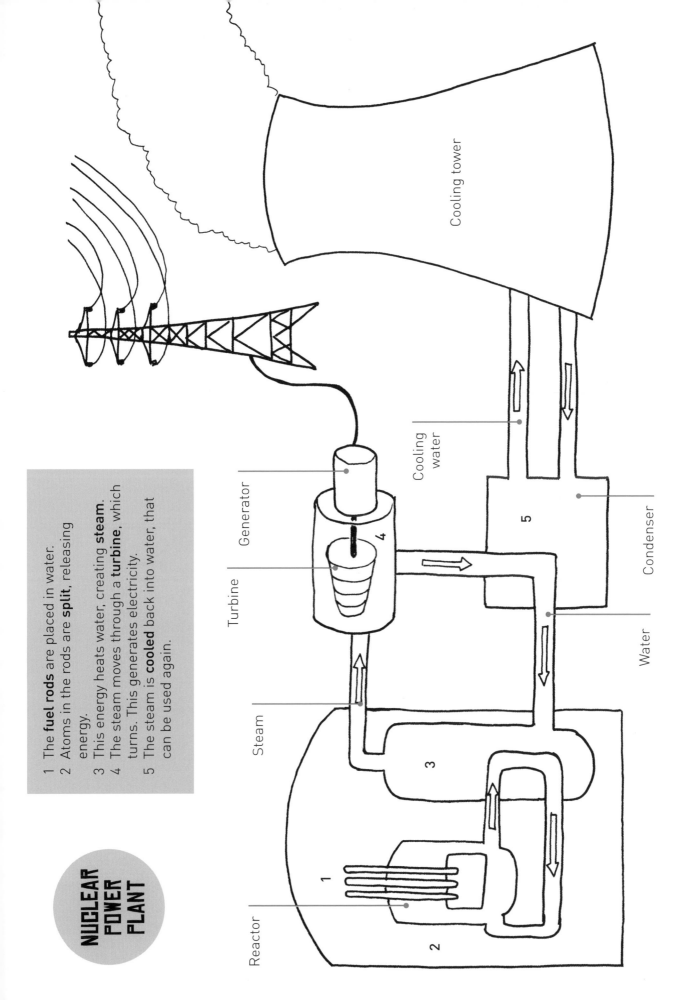

**NUCLEAR POWER PLANT**

1 The **fuel rods** are placed in water.
2 Atoms in the rods are **split**, releasing energy.
3 This energy heats water, creating **steam**.
4 The steam moves through a **turbine**, which turns. This generates electricity.
5 The steam is **cooled** back into water, that can be used again.

Cooling tower

Generator

Cooling water

Turbine

Condenser

Steam

Water

Reactor

# RENEWABLE ENERGY

When the Earth's oil, gas, and coal run out, people will need other sources of energy. Today, some buildings generate some of their own power. Solar panels attached to rooftops absorb the Sun's energy which is later used to heat water supplies.

Strong, steady winds can be put to work turning windmill blades. As the blades spin, they turn a shaft that generates electricity.

## QUICK FACTS

The principle of the **WINDMILL** has been known since ancient times.

The first solar **POWER STATION** was built in 1969 at Odeillo in France.

Modern wind turbines come in several shapes. Large groups of them are called **WIND FARMS**.

Many space **TELESCOPES** and craft use solar power.

If we could use just a small part of the **SUN'S** energy it would fulfil all the world's needs for power.

Many world **GOVERNMENTS** are committed to finding new sources of sustainable energy, such as solar power, hydropower, and wind power, as alternatives to fossil and nuclear energy.

Many houses nowadays have **solar panels** on the roof.

Wind farms consist of hundreds of huge **turbines** situated on windy hills.

# POLLUTION

Pollution is the name we give to waste products that enter the air, soil, and water, but cannot be quickly broken down naturally. The processes that cause most pollution are all man-made and involve emissions from factories and cars among other things. They affect the health of plants and animals, including humans, and the environments in which they live.

## QUICK FACTS

**EXHAUST FUMES** from motor vehicles are one of the main pollutants.

Sewage and waste from **INDUSTRY** are discharged into our rivers.

**FARMING** practises also pollute rivers and lakes with fertilizers and pesticides.

Rivers and canals are often used as unofficial **DUMPING** sites for household waste.

It is important, as far as possible, to use materials that can break down in the soil when they are thrown away. Such materials are said to be **BIODEGRADABLE**.

To improve matters, many countries have laws to protect our Earth. But we all need to help to keep the environment **CLEAN** and **HEALTHY**.

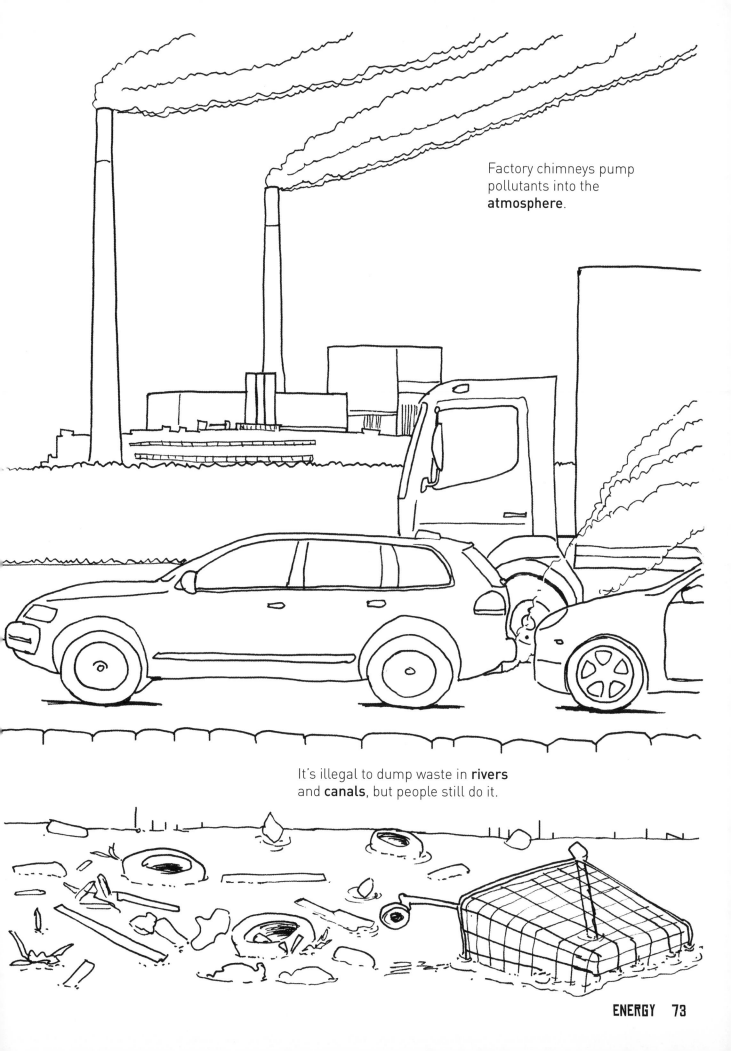

Factory chimneys pump pollutants into the **atmosphere**.

It's illegal to dump waste in **rivers** and **canals**, but people still do it.

# RECYCLING

Recycling is the process that reuses everyday waste, such as tins, glass containers, newspapers, and office paper. The process is designed to collect, process, and reuse materials instead of throwing them away. Recycling helps conserve raw materials and energy that manufacturers would otherwise use to make new products.

## QUICK FACTS

Recycling keeps materials out of **LANDFILLS** (areas where waste is deposited and covered with earth).

It also helps reduce the **POLLUTION** that may result from waste disposal.

Recycling programs also collect **GARDEN WASTE** and used **MOTOR OIL**.

It is very easy to recycle **GLASS**. It is simply broken up and melted, before being shaped again.

When you buy a new **CAR**, up to 40 per cent of the steel may have been recycled from old cars.

WHAT COLOR WOULD YOU USE FOR EACH KIND OF WASTE?

This is the **symbol** for recycling in many countries around the world.

In many places, **bins** for different kinds of recycling are manufactured in different colors.

# TRANSPORT

# GEARS

A gear is a mechanical device that transfers rotating motion and power from one part of a machine to another.

Gears are produced in a wide range of sizes, and they vary greatly in use. They span from the tiny gears that drive the hands of a watch to the huge gears that turn the propeller of a supertanker. A simple gear consists of a metal wheel or disc with slots called teeth around the edge.

## QUICK FACTS

--------------------------------------

Gears always work in **PAIRS**. The teeth of one gear fit together with the teeth of the other gear.

--------------------------------------

In fuel-powered vehicles, a gear has a metal **AXLE** in the middle. The axle of one gear is connected to a power source, such as an electric motor.

--------------------------------------

A **BICYCLE'S** gear system makes pedaling easier at certain times. Low gears, which make it easy to pedal up hills or against the wind, rotate the rear wheel only a little bit during each turn of the pedals.

--------------------------------------

Scottish **BLACKSMITH** Kirkpatrick Macmillan invented the bicycle in 1838.

--------------------------------------

When a pair of gears touch, they turn in **opposite** directions.

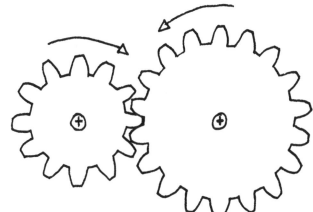

When a pair of gears are linked by a chain, they turn in **the same** direction.

A SIMPLE BICYCLE GEAR

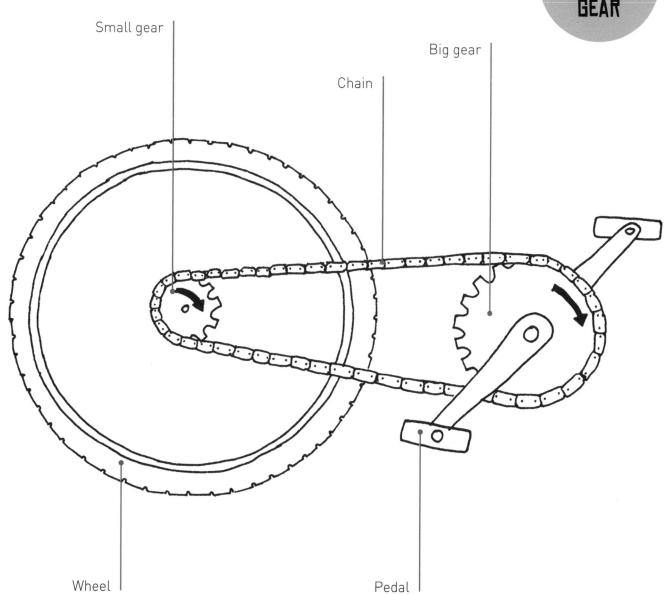

Small gear

Chain

Big gear

Wheel

Pedal

# ENGINES

An engine is a device for transforming heat from burned fuel into motive power. Steam engines are external combustion engines—the fuel is burned in a separate boiler (external from the engine) to make the steam that provides the motive force.

Internal combustion engines, such as gasoline (petrol) or diesel engines, burn their fuel inside their engines. Internal combustion engines are usually fueled by gasoline or diesel.

## QUICK FACTS

In 1885, German Gottlieb Daimler invented the gasoline engine when he developed a **CARBURETOR**—a device that allows an engine to burn a mix of air and gasoline.

The advantage of **GASOLINE** is that it is much easier to store than coal gas.

The **DIESEL** engine was invented by Rudolf Diesel in 1893.

It was intended to be an alternative to the oversized, expensive **STEAM** engines that were used in industry.

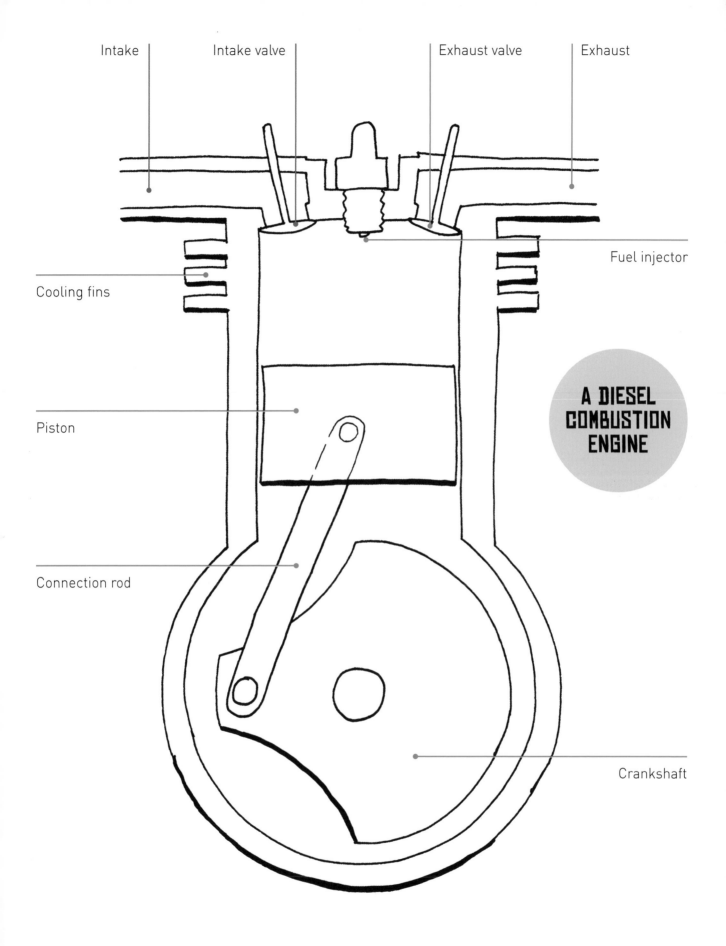

Intake

Intake valve

Exhaust valve

Exhaust

Fuel injector

Cooling fins

Piston

Connection rod

A DIESEL COMBUSTION ENGINE

Crankshaft

# CARS

The very first vehicle able to run on the open road was powered by steam. However, it was not until the development of the internal combustion engine in the second half of the 19th century that motor transport began to be successful.

In a car, the engine also powers an alternator which generates electrical current. This current is stored in the battery, and is used for the car's lights, windscreen wipers, radio, and other features such as electric windows.

## QUICK FACTS

Most gasoline (petrol) engines are quite **NOISY**, and give off harmful fumes.

Quieter and cleaner electric cars are being designed. However, their batteries need continually **RECHARGING**.

A **CATALYTIC CONVERTOR** is a device that reduces the exhaust pollutants produced by a car's engine.

In 1913, the American Model T Ford became the first affordable, **MASS-PRODUCED** car.

CARS HAVE CHANGED A LOT SINCE THEY WERE INVENTED IN THE LATE 1800S.

1890s

1920s

1970s

2010s

# FLIGHT

As an aeroplane flies, the air passes over the surface of its wings. These wings are shaped with a curved top surface and a flatter lower surface, which means that air passing over the top of the wing has to travel a little faster than that below the wing. This causes the pressure to lower above the wing, while the air pressure below pushes up. The end result is the lift that keeps the aeroplane in the air.

## QUICK FACTS

**JET** engines propel a plane just like a rocket, with a stream of hot gases.

A plane with no engine is called a **GLIDER**.

During the late 18th century, people made the first flights in the air using **BALLOONS**.

In 1903, the American Wright brothers made the first successful **POWERED** aeroplane flights in history.

Concorde was a **SUPERSONIC** airliner. The sonic "boom" it produced, together with noise and air pollution concerns, has limited the development of such aircraft.

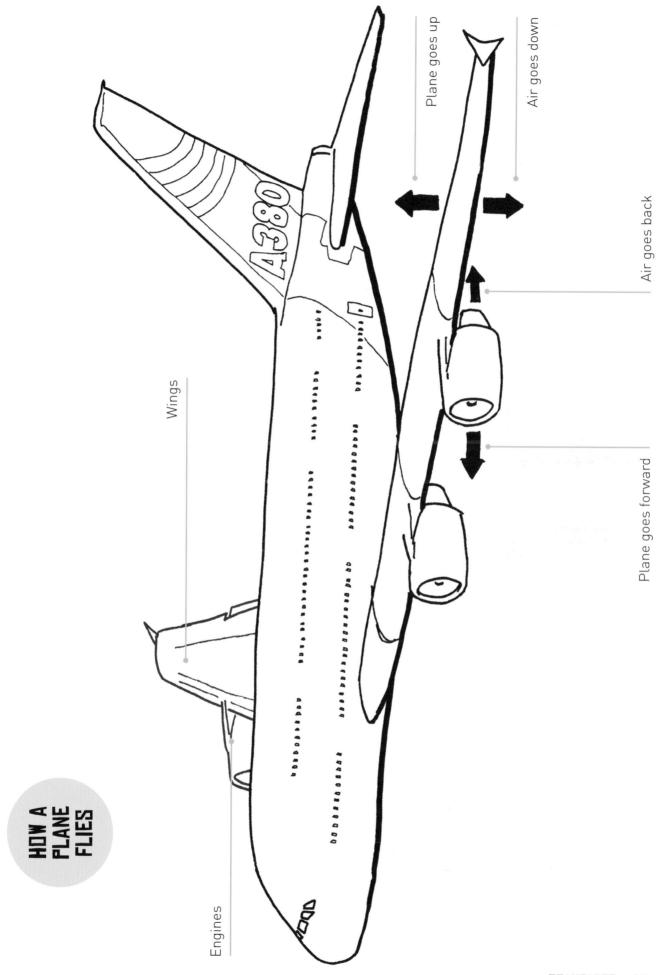

HOW A
PLANE
FLIES

Plane goes up

Air goes down

Air goes back

Plane goes forward

Wings

Engines

# BOATS

A boat floats on water because the fluid itself holds it up.

The upward push on a floating object is called "buoyancy".
If you want to feel this force, just push a blown-up beach ball
into water. You will feel the water push up on the ball.

When a solid object is placed in liquid it pushes some of the fluid
aside. If it weighs less than the water it pushes aside, it floats.

If the solid is less dense than the fluid, it will float.
A boat contains large quantities of air, and so is less dense than water.

## QUICK FACTS

------------------------------------------

In about 2900 BCE, the Egyptians began to build boats
with **SAILS**, which used wind power to propel the craft.

------------------------------------------

Early sailors in **WOODEN** sailing ships were constantly at
the mercy of the winds, and high seas.

------------------------------------------

During the 19th century, technological **INNOVATIONS**
such as iron hulls, and steam engines, made shipping
faster, safer, and more reliable.

------------------------------------------

Modern ships have **ENGINES**, but sailing is still a popular
leisure activity, requiring a lot of skill.

------------------------------------------

The **HOVERCRAFT** was invented in 1955 by British
scientist Christopher Cockerell.

------------------------------------------

BOATS TODAY COME IN MANY SHAPES AND SIZES.

# INVENTIONS

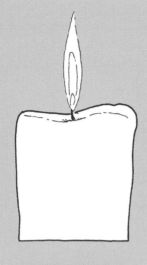

# FIRE

Fire is a chemical reaction that occurs very quickly, and gives off heat and light. The most common is the reaction between oxygen and a fuel. If heat and light are given off, you have a fire.

Fire has been known to humans since the earliest times.

## QUICK FACTS

Archaeologists have found evidence of **CHARCOAL** and charred remains dating back thousands of years.

Early humans discovered how to make fire by using a simple wooden stick called a **FIRE DRILL**.

The first safety **MATCHES** were made in Sweden in 1844, using non-poisonous red phosphorous.

Every **FUEL** has its own particular temperature at which it begins to burn. This temperature is called the **FLASH POINT** of the fuel.

**FIREPROOF** clothing is often shiny, because this helps to reflect the radiated heat away from the body.

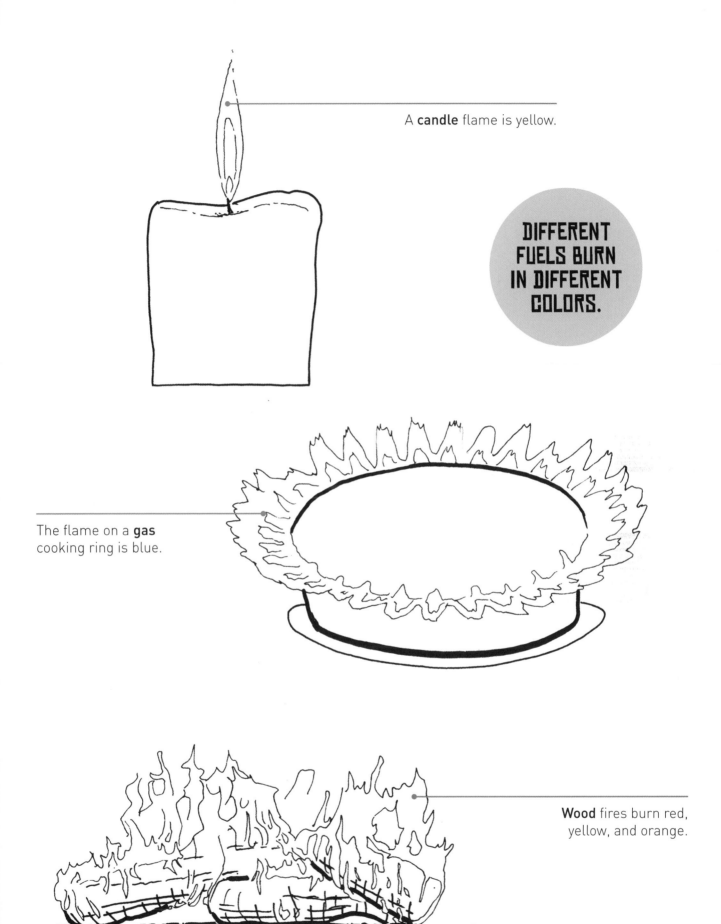

A **candle** flame is yellow.

DIFFERENT FUELS BURN IN DIFFERENT COLORS.

The flame on a **gas** cooking ring is blue.

**Wood** fires burn red, yellow, and orange.

# CLOCKS

Over the centuries, humans have measured time
in very different ways. Here are some of them.

----------------------------------------

The first **SUNDIALS** were probably just poles stuck into
the ground, with stones placed around the pole to mark
the position of the shadow.

----------------------------------------

**CANDLE** clocks were used in the ninth century.

----------------------------------------

An **HOURGLASS** tells time by means of sand trickling
through a narrow opening.

----------------------------------------

A **WATER CLOCK** measures time by allowing water to drip
slowly from one marked container into another.

----------------------------------------

By the 1700s, people had developed **CLOCKWORK** clocks,
and watches that told time to the minute.

----------------------------------------

**DIGITAL** clocks contain electronic circuits which receive
digital signals. The clocks receive the signals in binary
code which it can understand.

----------------------------------------

**ATOMIC** clocks can measure time precisely, to the tiniest
fragment of a second.

----------------------------------------

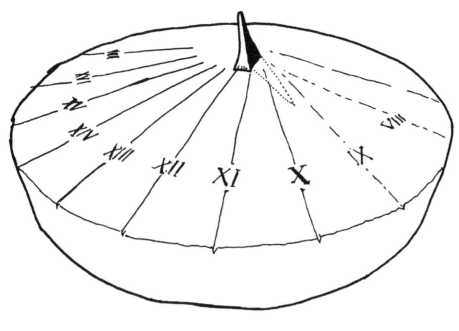

CLOCKS HAVE CHANGED A LOT OVER THE CENTURIES.

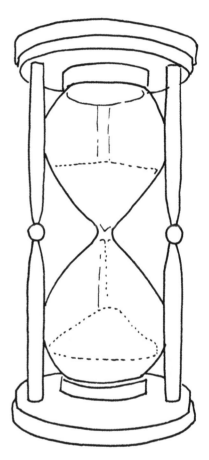

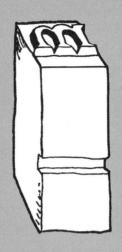

# PRINTING

In about 1450, a German named Johannes Gutenberg
built the first true printing press.

Using movable metal blocks like the one shown above, Gutenberg was
able to make exact copies of books very cheaply. The first books he printed
were the Bible and other religious works. Soon other printers started, and
by 1500 they were producing many different sorts of literature, including
poems and stories. For the first time, books were available to everyone.

## QUICK FACTS

The first books were made about 4,000 years ago by the
Egyptians, who took flattened layers of **PAPYRUS** stems
to make sheets.

Printing used to need a separate small **METAL BLOCK** for
every single letter.

American Joseph Gayetty is credited with inventing
**TOILET PAPER** in 1857. Before Gayetty's invention, people
tore pages out of mail-order catalogs.

The first **INKJET** printer was invented in 1964.

Nowadays we produce **WOOD-FREE** paper in an attempt
to limit the damage to our environment.

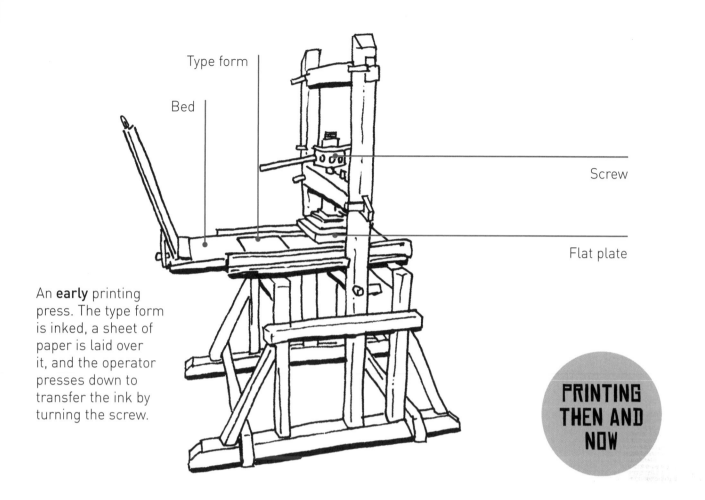

Type form

Bed

Screw

Flat plate

An **early** printing press. The type form is inked, a sheet of paper is laid over it, and the operator presses down to transfer the ink by turning the screw.

**PRINTING THEN AND NOW**

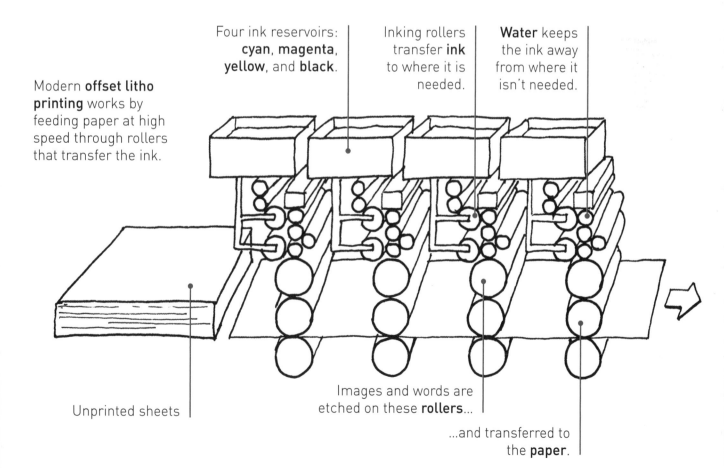

Four ink reservoirs: **cyan**, **magenta**, **yellow**, and **black**.

Inking rollers transfer **ink** to where it is needed.

**Water** keeps the ink away from where it isn't needed.

Modern **offset litho printing** works by feeding paper at high speed through rollers that transfer the ink.

Unprinted sheets

Images and words are etched on these **rollers**...

...and transferred to the **paper**.

# LENSES

A lens is a curved piece of glass that focuses light on a particular area.

If your eye is not exactly the right shape, or its lens cannot focus properly, you cannot form a clear image on the retina (inside your eye).

A long-sighted person can see things in the distance while nearby objects are blurred. They need glasses with concave lenses. A short-sighted person can see nearby objects very clearly while distant ones are blurred. They need glasses with convex lenses.

## QUICK FACTS

A **CONVEX** lens has a shape that curves outward.
A **CONCAVE** lens has a surface that curves inward.

Many people prefer **CONTACT LENSES** to glasses. They are thin plastic discs that rest on the surface of the eye.

A **MICROSCOPE** is an instrument that uses lenses to help us see tiny things that are invisible to the naked eye.

Some microscopes are so powerful they can **MAGNIFY** the smallest objects many thousands of times.

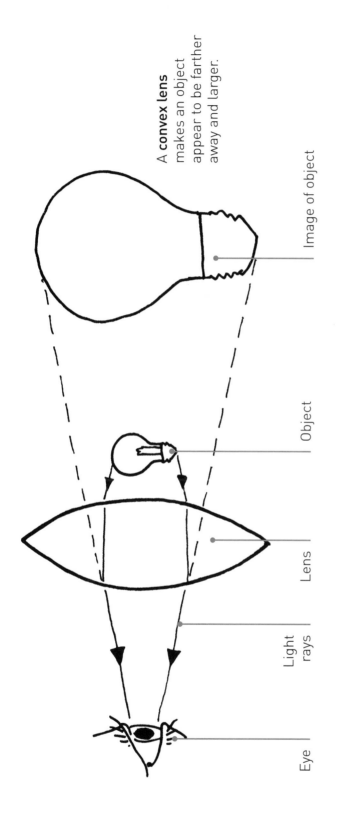

A **convex lens** makes an object appear to be farther away and larger.

Image of object

Object

Lens

Light rays

Eye

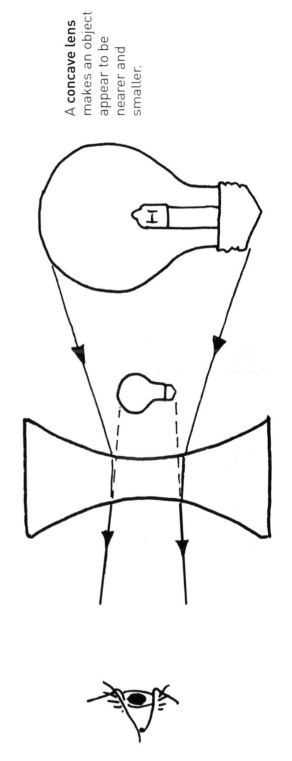

A **concave lens** makes an object appear to be nearer and smaller.

# THE INDUSTRIAL REVOLUTION

One of the biggest changes in the history of the world, the Industrial Revolution, started in Europe in the 1700s.

Britain was the first home of many new machines, new types of materials, and new ways of making power. This was the age of coal and iron, of gas and electricity, of railways and factories. The new inventions soon spread to America and Europe.

## QUICK FACTS

As industry **EXPANDED**, greater loads of heavy goods such as coal and iron had to be taken across country.

Rivers did not always go the right way, so **CANALS** were dug. The first modern canal system opened in France in 1681, and was copied later in the UK and USA.

In 1837, the **GREAT WESTERN**, the first all-steam ship to carry passengers across the Atlantic, was launched.

Raw **COTTON**, grown mainly in the USA, was very difficult and slow to clean. Whitney's cotton gin was a simple machine that brushed out seeds from cotton.

**Isambard Kingdom Brunel**
was a famous engineer
and bridge-builder.

**Eli Whitney** improved the
process of harvesting cotton.

**George Stephenson**
developed the steam
engine for use in trains.

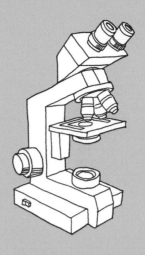

# TELESCOPES

Telescopes help us to see far into the distance.

Refracting telescopes work by having a convex lens which bends light rays from an object to form an upside-down image of the object. A second lens, the eyepiece, bends the rays again and magnifies the image.

A reflecting telescope uses a shaped primary mirror to reflect light to a smaller secondary mirror. The light is then reflected to the focus and the image is viewed through an eyepiece.

## QUICK FACTS

Dutch spectacle-maker Hans Lippershey is credited with **INVENTING** the refracting telescope in 1608.

Galileo is credited with having developed telescopes for **ASTRONOMICAL** observation in 1609.

Special **SOLAR** telescopes have been constructed so that the intensity of the image of the Sun will not damage the observer's eye.

Radio observatories have radio telescopes for the study of **RADIO WAVES**.

**MICROSCOPES** (see above) show us tiny things, close up.

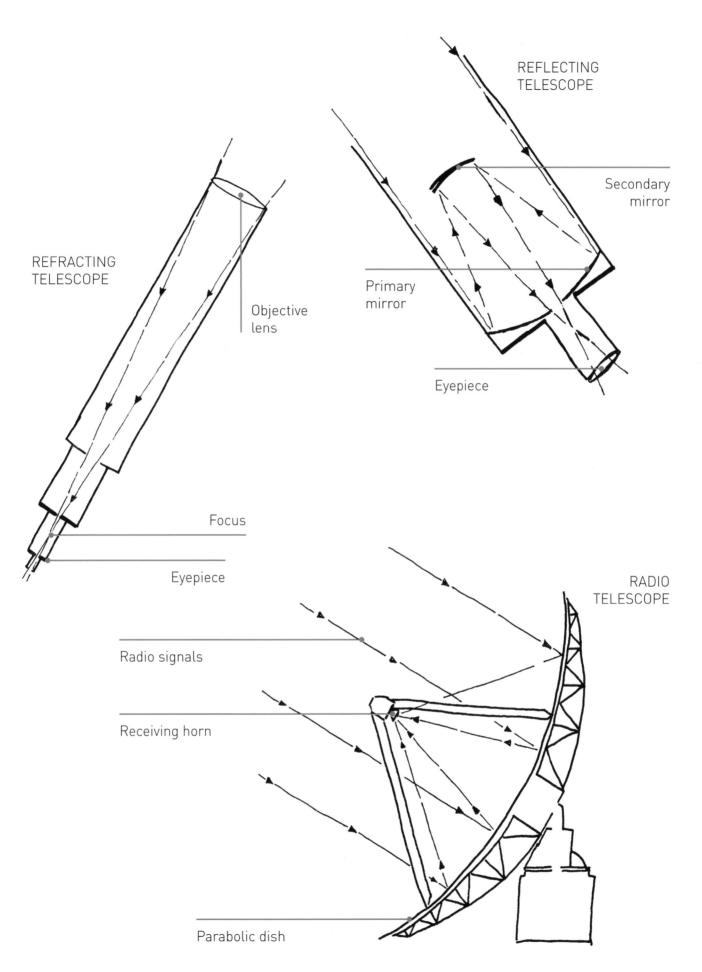

REFLECTING
TELESCOPE

Secondary
mirror

Primary
mirror

Eyepiece

REFRACTING
TELESCOPE

Objective
lens

Focus

Eyepiece

Radio signals

Receiving horn

RADIO
TELESCOPE

Parabolic dish

# PLASTICS

The word plastic literally means "capable of being molded or modeled". When heated, plastics are somewhat like modeling clay. This is what gives them their name.

Plastics have many unique properties that make them very useful for special purposes. They resist the flow of electricity, they are light in weight, and they wear extremely well. It is also possible to make them unbreakable.

## QUICK FACTS

------------------------------------------------

Plastics replaced a range of traditional materials used in **INDUSTRY**, such as wood, metal, glass, ceramics, natural fibers, ivory, and bone.

------------------------------------------------

A toy duck is a good example of how easily plastic can be **MOLDED**.

------------------------------------------------

The **SPACE** technology of the late 1960s, among other developments, has been applied by scientists to develop new plastics and other synthetic materials.

------------------------------------------------

There is at least **20 TIMES** more plastic produced today than 20 years ago!

------------------------------------------------

THOUSANDS OF ITEMS WE USE IN DAILY LIFE ARE MADE OF PLASTIC.

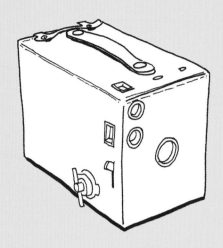

# CAMERAS

When we open and close the shutter of a traditional camera, light comes in and strikes the film. A chemical reaction then takes place on the film. It is taken out of the camera and treated with more chemicals to make the print visible, and prevent further changes when exposed to light.

Digital cameras are a recent development. They convert the images they receive into electrical signals.

## QUICK FACTS

The human **EYE** is actually a form of camera. When you look around, your eyes "take pictures" of the things that you see.

**INSECTS'** extraordinary eyes are made up of hundreds of tiny lenses. The images from all the lenses are processed by the insect's brain.

The Kodak Brownie (see above), launched in 1900, was the first camera that was **AFFORDABLE** for ordinary people.

The first **CAMERA PHONE**, the J-SH04, was sold in Japan in 2000.

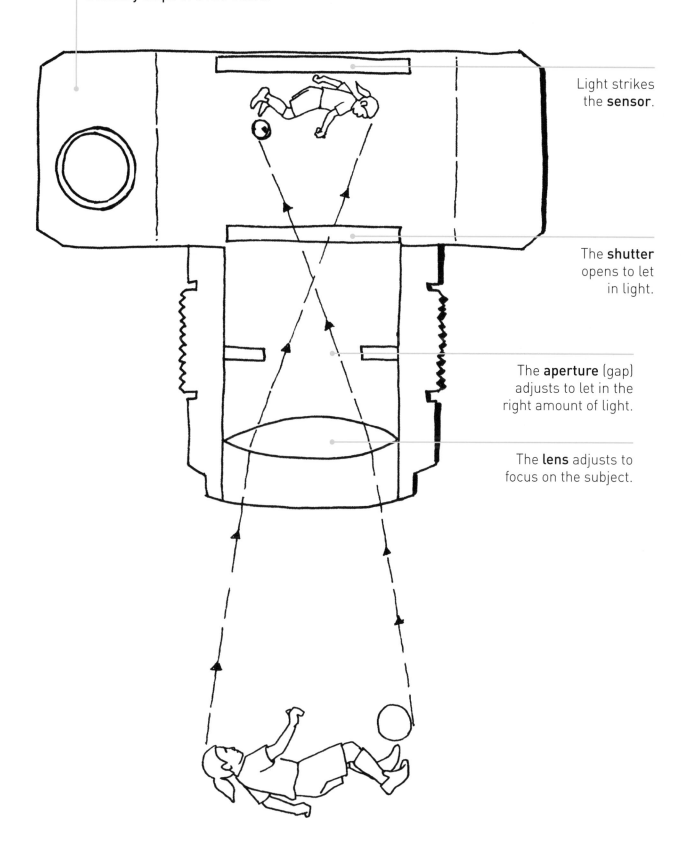

Image data is stored on **memory chips** in a RAM card.

Light strikes the **sensor**.

The **shutter** opens to let in light.

The **aperture** (gap) adjusts to let in the right amount of light.

The **lens** adjusts to focus on the subject.

# TELEPHONES

Landline telephones transmit speech messages
along wires by means of electrical signals.

Cellphones (mobile phones) are two-way radios that convert the sound
to radio waves, which travel through the air until they reach a receiver.

## QUICK FACTS

The Scottish-born American inventor Alexander
Graham Bell **INVENTED** the telephone in 1876.

The first words **SPOKEN** down a telephone were,
"Mr Watson, come here, I want you!" Bell was testing
out his invention when he spilt some chemicals on his
clothes, and called to his assistant for help.

Light travels much faster than electricity, and it is used
in **OPTICAL** cables to carry sound for very long distances
without electrical interference.

Cellphone **A** calls Cellphone B.

Cellphone A scans the network to find a **base station**.

The **base station** transmits the signal on to the switching center.

The switching center locates a **base station** near cellphone B.

**Cellphone B** receives the call.

# RADIO

Radio signals are transmitted using carrier waves. Those with the longest wave lengths are bounced very long distances off the ionosphere (far up in the sky). A radio transmitter changes the radio wave to convey information.

Digital radio works in the same way, but instead of sending out one signal, stations send out a bundle of signals.

## QUICK FACTS

The portable radio was invented in 1947. The invention was made possible by the development of a device called a **TRANSISTOR**, which replaced the valves inside radios that picked up radio signals.

On October 18 1954 the world's "first **POCKET** radio" went on sale. The Regency TR1 is just 4.75 in. high.

In 1991, British inventor Trevor Baylis invented a portable **WIND-UP** radio.

**FIREFIGHTERS** need radios to be in constant communication with main control, and with each other.

RADIO SETS HAVE CHANGED A LOT OVER THE YEARS.

1920s

1950s

1980s

In the **2010s**, people can listen to radio on their computers.

# TELEVISION

The television was invented by John Logie Baird in the 1920s. Until then, most scientists had considered such a system to be impossible.

Baird realized that pictures could be sent by radio if the images were broken down into a series of electronic impulses. He invented a mechanical scanner that, by 1926, was able to scan and transmit moving images.

## QUICK FACTS

Baird also demonstrated **COLOR** television, in 1928.

A **TRANSISTOR** is a tiny device that controls the flow of electric current. It's used in radios, TVs, and computers.

Radio waves generate weak currents in a radio or TV antenna. Transistors **AMPLIFY** these signals.

21st-century technology has brought **DIGITAL** television, and flat-screen interactive television sets.

With the use of communication **SATELLITES**, TV programs can be beamed to the most remote parts of the world, including the Amazon jungle!

TELEVISION SETS HAVE CHANGED A LOT OVER THE YEARS.

1940s

1970s

1990s

2010s

# COMPUTERS

A computer is a piece of equipment for processing information very rapidly and accurately. It processes words, pictures, sounds, and numbers. Some computers can make billions of calculations per second.

New data can be inputted into a computer from the keyboard or downloaded via a memory stick or DVD drive, or from the internet.

## QUICK FACTS

The heart of a computer is a **MICROPROCESSOR** which contains millions of tiny electronic devices on a chip.

Other silicon chips form the computer's **MEMORY**, where information is stored until it is needed.

Any modern electrical device needs a huge number of **CONNECTIONS** to join together all the small components needed for it to work effectively.

Printed **CIRCUITS** are complex electrical circuits that are literally photographed on to a layer of material.

On a **TABLET** computer, a touchscreen has replaced the computer mouse and keyboard.

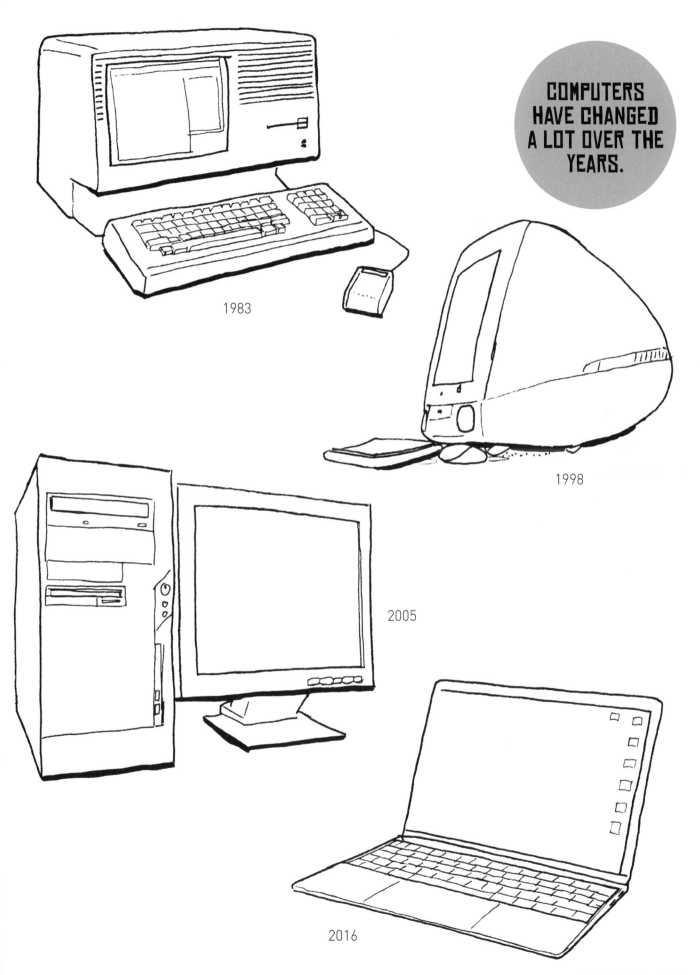

COMPUTERS HAVE CHANGED A LOT OVER THE YEARS.

1983

1998

2005

2016

# THE INTERNET

The Internet is a worldwide collection of computers connected by cables, telephone lines, and satellites.

The Internet allows people to send messages (emails) to anyone else who is connected, interact with other computer users wherever they are in the world, and look at information via the World Wide Web.

## QUICK FACTS

In 1971, American computer scientist Ray Tomlinson devised a computer program for sending messages on the ARPAnet network. This would become **EMAIL**.

Englishman Tim Berners-Lee invented the **WORLD WIDE WEB** in 1989.

The Apple **IMAC** was launched in 1998. With just two steps needed to set up Internet access, it revolutionized home computing.

By the mid-1990s, **MILLIONS** of computers all around the world were connected to the web.

It first became possible to listen to **MUSIC** online in 1995.

Some people do **homework**.

Others enjoy **chatting**.

Some people try to **sell** you things online!

THE INTERNET CONNECTS PEOPLE AROUND THE WORLD.

You can watch **movies** or read **stories** online.

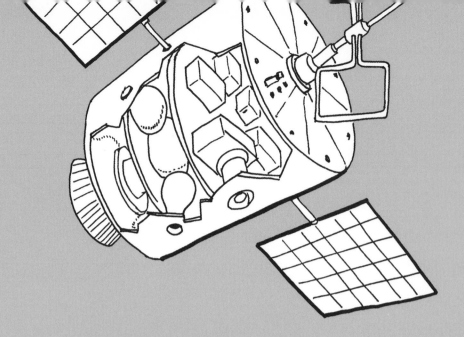

# SATELLITES

Communication satellites receive signals beamed at them from the Earth, and send them on to other places. They transmit television and telephone signals around the world, even to remote areas.

They are also used for defense communications, including checking on the movement of military forces. Satellites can survey the surface of the Earth, and track hurricanes. They can also help to examine resources such as crops, forests, and even minerals.

## QUICK FACTS

Some satellites survey the Earth's surface so that we can give a more accurate **WEATHER** forecast.

**NAVIGATION** satellites enable people on land or at sea to work out their exact map position to within a few feet.

**GEOSTATIONARY** satellites can be positioned right over the areas where they are needed. They can be used for spying, because they remain over just one area.

Satellites orbiting the Earth must travel at high speed to escape being brought down by the Earth's **GRAVITY**.

Command
antenna

Communication
antenna

Batteries

Solar panels

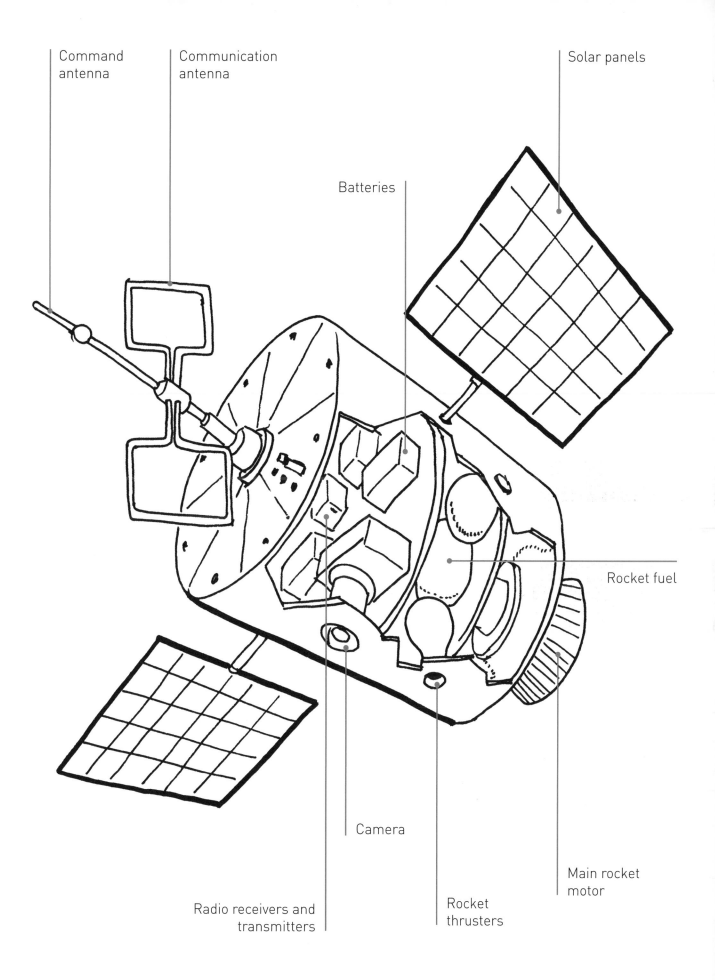

Rocket fuel

Camera

Radio receivers and
transmitters

Rocket
thrusters

Main rocket
motor

# FOOD

Humans need a variety of different elements in their food to stay healthy.

In general, wholegrain starchy foods are better for us than than those that have been heavily processed. For example, brown bread is in general healthier for us than white. Fast food is often high in calories, fat, and cholesterol, and should be eaten in moderation.

## QUICK FACTS

**SUGARS** are substances that plants use to store energy, and are known as simple carbohydrates, because they can be broken down in the human body quickly.

Starches are complex carbohydrates that the body takes longer to absorb. They provide **ENERGY** for many hours.

The first **BREAD** was made in Neolithic times, nearly 12,000 years ago. It probably consisted of coarsely crushed grain mixed with water, which was then laid on hot stones.

Today, because we know that too much fat and sugar are bad for us, scientists are hard at work making our favorite treats **HEALTHIER**.

Nevertheless, there are more than 300,000 **FAST FOOD** restaurants in the United States alone!

# A BALANCED DIET

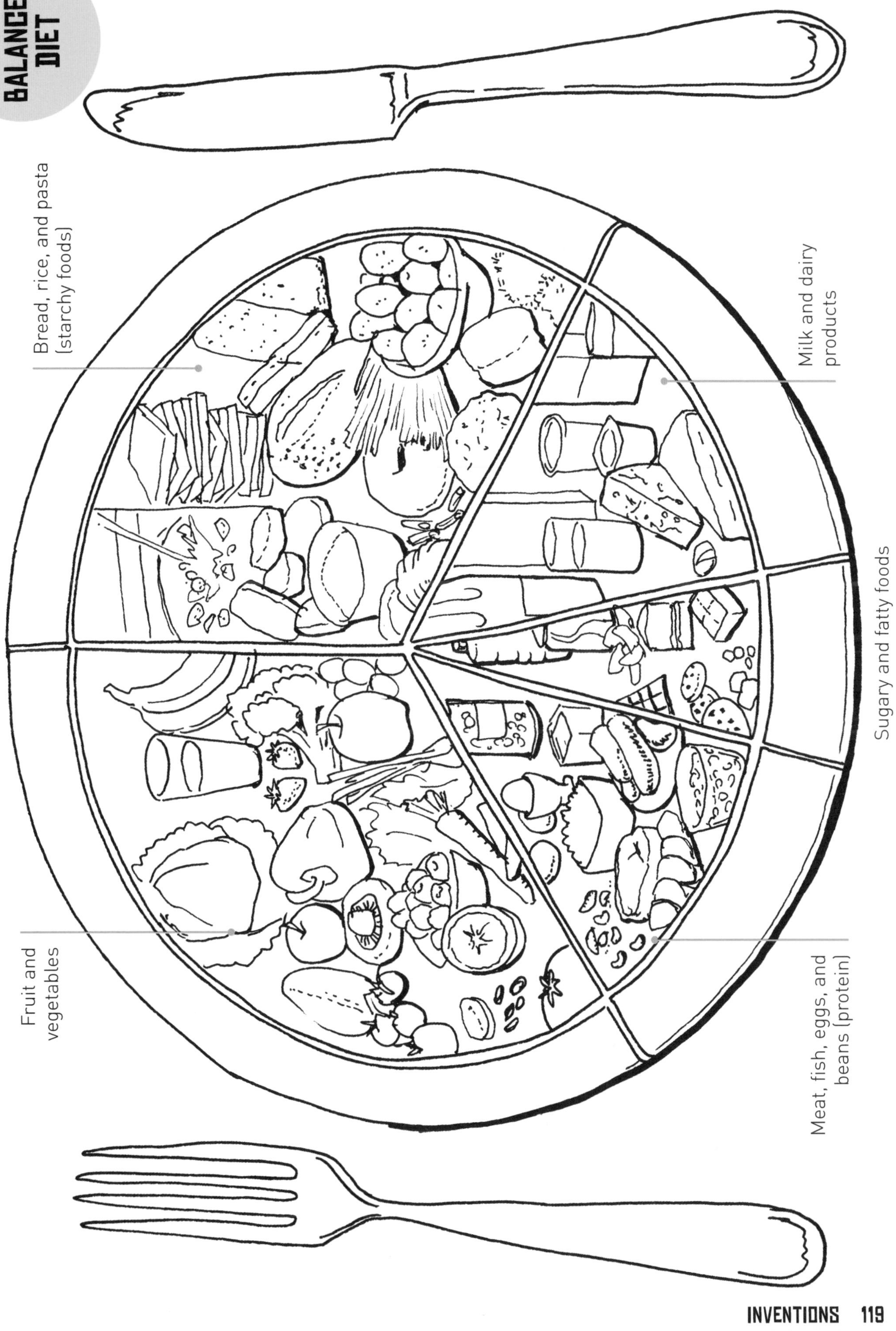
Bread, rice, and pasta (starchy foods)
Milk and dairy products
Sugary and fatty foods
Meat, fish, eggs, and beans (protein)
Fruit and vegetables

# ANCIENT INVENTIONS

Many of the things we think of as utterly basic and essential now were cutting-edge innovations once!

**SCALES** (c.4000 BCE): Simple scales (a length of wood or metal balanced with pans hung from each end) are first developed in Mesopotamia.

**BRICKS** (c.3500 BCE): In the Middle East bricks are made from clay, then fired in a kiln to make them hard and waterproof. Before this, bricks were made from mud and straw, and sometimes dissolved in heavy rain!

**COTTON** (c.3000 BCE): Cotton cloth is invented when the people of the Indus Valley (in modern-day Pakistan) find out that the fibers attached to the cotton plant seeds can be woven into a fine fabric.

**CHAIRS** (c.2600 BCE): The ancient Egyptians use chairs with padded seats and four legs.

**INK** (c.2500 BCE): Ink for writing is made from soot mixed with glue.

**WHEEL SPOKES** (c.2000 BCE): Mesopotamian craftsmen begin to produce wheels with a rim, hub, and spokes instead of the heavy, solid plank used previously.

**CHOCOLATE** (c.1000 BCE): is made from cocoa beans. It is believed that the Olmec Indians of Central America were the first to grow cocoa beans as a crop.

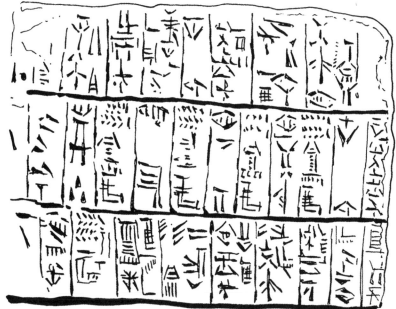

A Mesopotamian **brick** with engravings.

An Egyptian drawing showing the use of **scales**.

Olmec art showing **drinking chocolate** being used in a ceremony.

# 19TH-CENTURY INVENTIONS

The Victorian period saw many technological advances.

**BICYCLE** (1817): The "draisienne", invented by Baron Karl von Drais de Sauerbrun, is the first two-wheeled rider-propelled machine. "Velocipede" becomes its popular name. The wooden machine is propelled by the seated rider paddling their feet on the ground.

**REFRIGERATOR** (1844): American doctor John Gorrie builds a machine that uses compressed air to provide a cooling breeze for feverish patients in his hospital.

**SAFETY PIN** (1849): US mechanic Walter Hunt invents the modern safety pin. His design is actually very similar to one invented and worn by people 2,000 years ago.

**DYNAMITE** (1866): Swedish chemist Alfred Nobel invents an explosive that is safe to handle. Dynamite becomes widely used in the mining and construction industries.

**TOILET** (c.1880s): The flush toilet was first thought of in the 1500s, but Thomas Crapper designed the version we know today.

**TOOTHPASTE IN A TUBE** (1892): Crème Dentifrice, produced by US dentist Washington Sheffield, is the first toothpaste sold in tubes.

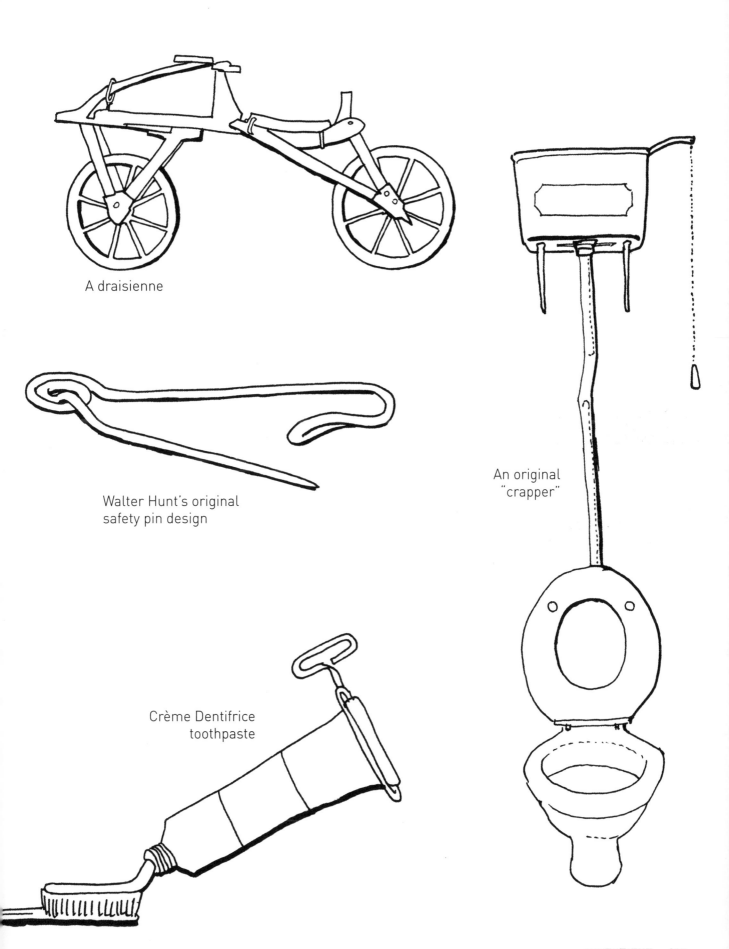

A draisienne

Walter Hunt's original
safety pin design

Crème Dentifrice
toothpaste

An original
"crapper"

# 20TH-CENTURY INVENTIONS

Life got a lot more comfortable thanks to some
of the innovations of the last century.

------------------------------------------------

**WASHING MACHINE** (1907): US inventor Alva Fisher invents
the first electric washing machine. The machine has
a drum that tumbles the clothes and water around.

------------------------------------------------

**MARS BAR** (1911): Frank Mars invents the "Mars bar"
when he comes up with the idea of producing
malted chocolate milkshakes in a solid form.

------------------------------------------------

**STICKY TAPE** (1925): By coating cellophane with glue,
US engineer Richard Drew produces Scotch Tape.

------------------------------------------------

**MICROWAVE OVEN** (1945): US engineer Percy LeBron
Spencer invents the microwave oven. While working on
radar, Spencer had made the discovery that powerful
microwaves had melted some candy in his pocket!

------------------------------------------------

**KEVLAR** (1960s): Kevlar, which is used in bullet-resistant
vests and crash helmets, is developed by US chemist
Stephanie Kwolek.

------------------------------------------------

**BAGLESS VACUUM CLEANER** (c.1978): UK inventor James
Dyson notices that the dust bags in conventional vacuum
cleaners clog up quickly. A few years later, he markets
a bagless cleaner.

------------------------------------------------

Early washing machine

1950s microwave

Early Mars bar wrapper design

Kevlar body armor

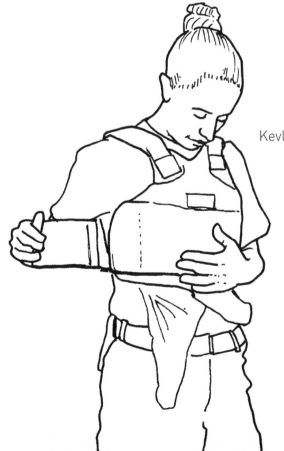

Scotch tape

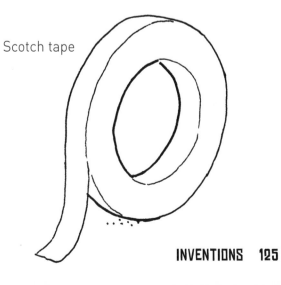

# THE HUMAN BODY

# YOUR BODY

Every organ in the human body works as part of a team,
to keep you going, and make you who you are.

You breathe air through
your **lungs**. These filter
oxygen into your blood.

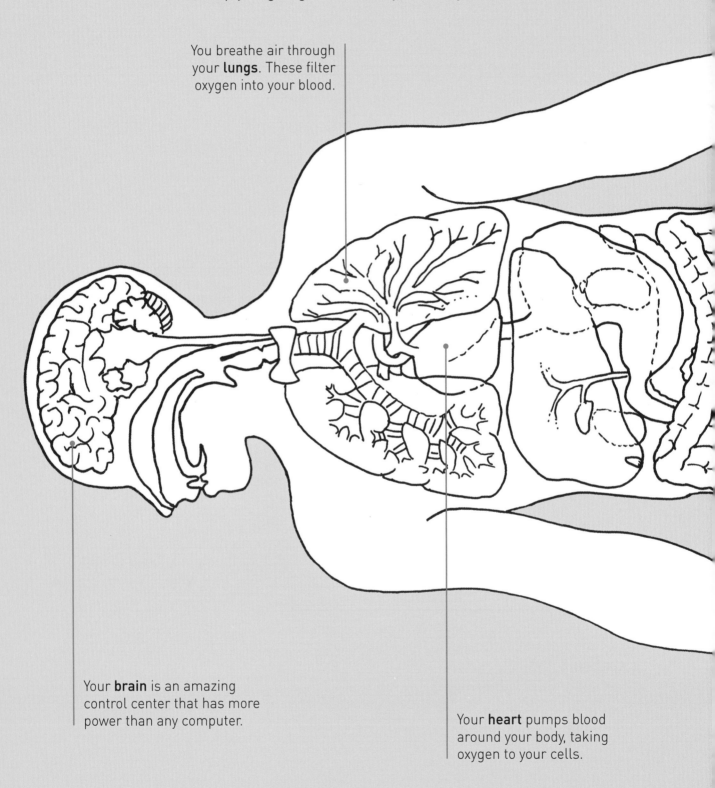

Your **brain** is an amazing
control center that has more
power than any computer.

Your **heart** pumps blood
around your body, taking
oxygen to your cells.

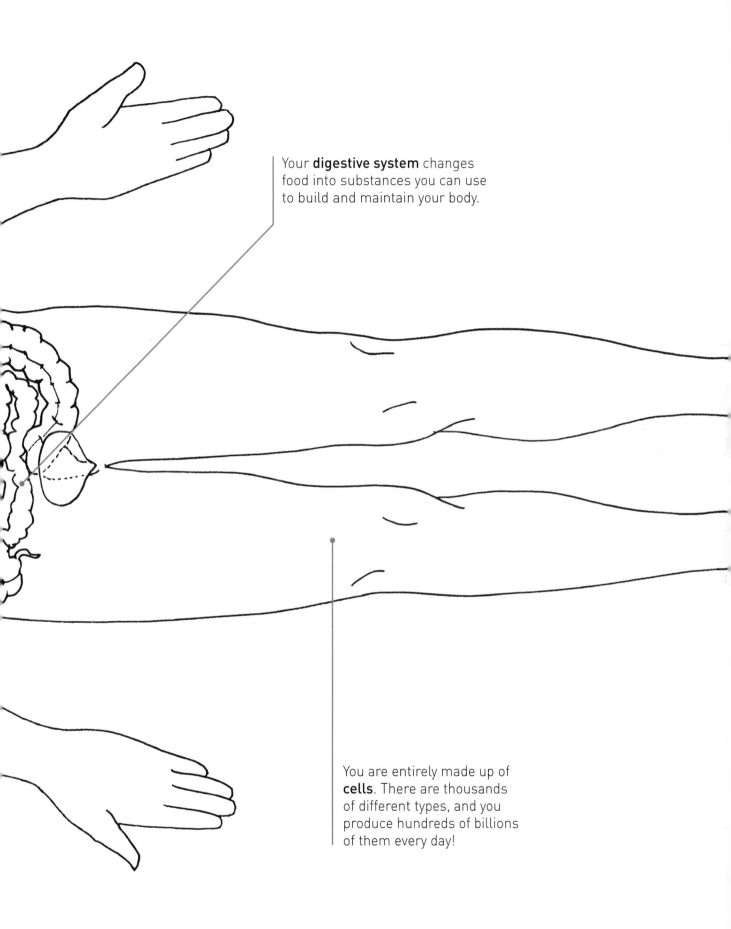

Your **digestive system** changes food into substances you can use to build and maintain your body.

You are entirely made up of **cells**. There are thousands of different types, and you produce hundreds of billions of them every day!

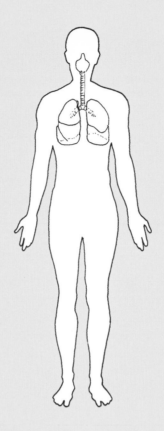

# YOUR SYSTEMS

Every part of your body is fed and supported by a complex network of interacting parts that hold your organs in place and keep them working.

## QUICK FACTS

Arteries, Veins, and Capillaries are **TINY TUBES** that carry your blood around your body.

Your rigid **SKELETON** keeps you standing.

Your skull is extremely thick and protects your **BRAIN** from bumps and bruises.

Muscles are flexible bundles of **FIBER** that pull on bones so that you can move.

**TENDONS** attach your muscles to your bones.

Nerves carry **MESSAGES** from your body to your brain.

Your **TEETH** are the hardest part of your body, and will last a lifetime if you look after them properly.

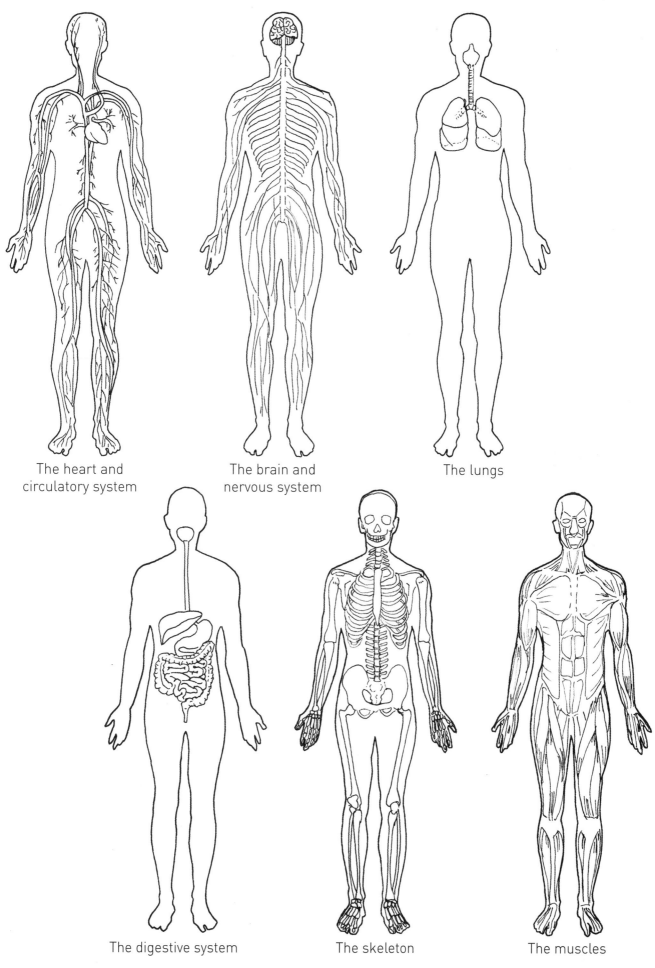

The heart and
circulatory system

The brain and
nervous system

The lungs

The digestive system

The skeleton

The muscles

# YOUR SENSES

Humans have five senses: sight, hearing, smell, taste, and touch. They help us to seek food and avoid danger, and alert us to problems like cold or injuries.

## QUICK FACTS

The human eye is so **SENSITIVE** that a person sitting on top of a hill on a moonless night could see a match being struck up to 50 miles away.

Most of your ear is **INSIDE** your skull. The visible part is just a flap of cartilage (gristle).

Most people are able to pick out about **4,000** different smells.

Your tongue can detect five different basic **FLAVORS**: salt, sour, sweet, bitter, and umami.

The skin on your **FINGERTIPS** is the most sensitive on your body.

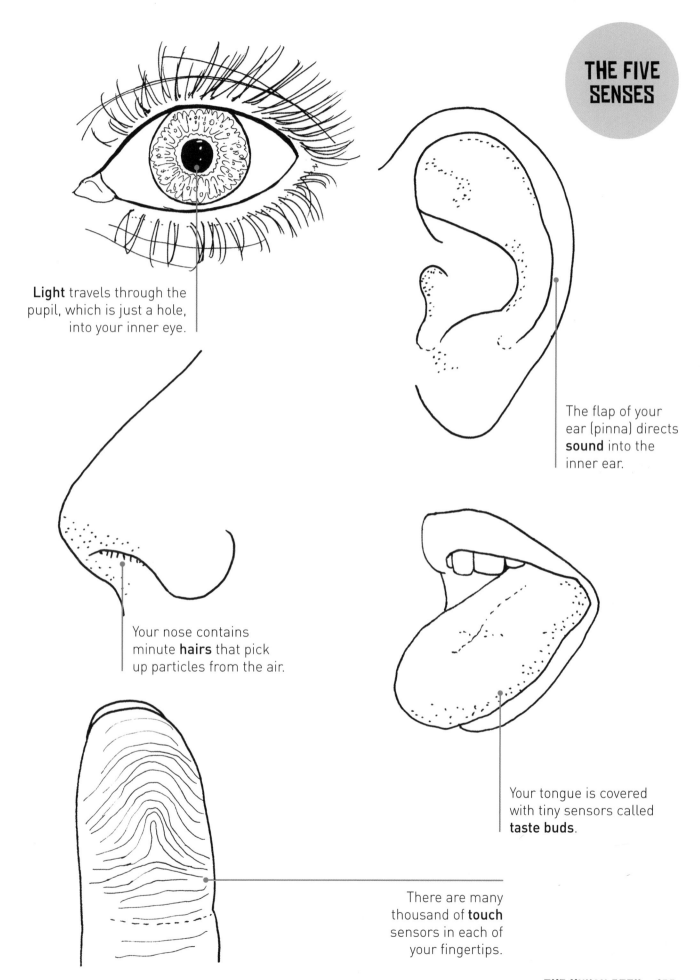

**Light** travels through the
pupil, which is just a hole,
into your inner eye.

The flap of your
ear (pinna) directs
**sound** into the
inner ear.

Your nose contains
minute **hairs** that pick
up particles from the air.

Your tongue is covered
with tiny sensors called
**taste buds**.

There are many
thousand of **touch**
sensors in each of
your fingertips.

# SPACE

# THE SOLAR SYSTEM

# OUR SUN

The Sun is the center of the Solar System. All the planets and asteroids are held in their orbits by its immense gravity. It also attracts comets.

For billions of years the Sun has been providing Earth with light that green plants use as an energy source. Herbivorous animals eat the plants, carnivorous animals eat the herbivores, and in this way the Sun powers life on Earth—including our own.

## QUICK FACTS

The Sun is about **109 TIMES** the diameter of Earth.

It is about **170,000 MILES** across.

Its **MASS** is about two billion billion billion tons.

Its average surface **TEMPERATURE** is 338°F.
The maximum is 10,500°F.

The Sun is about 93,000,000 miles from Earth. As light travels at the rate of 186,000 miles a second it takes **EIGHT MINUTES** for the light from the Sun to reach us.

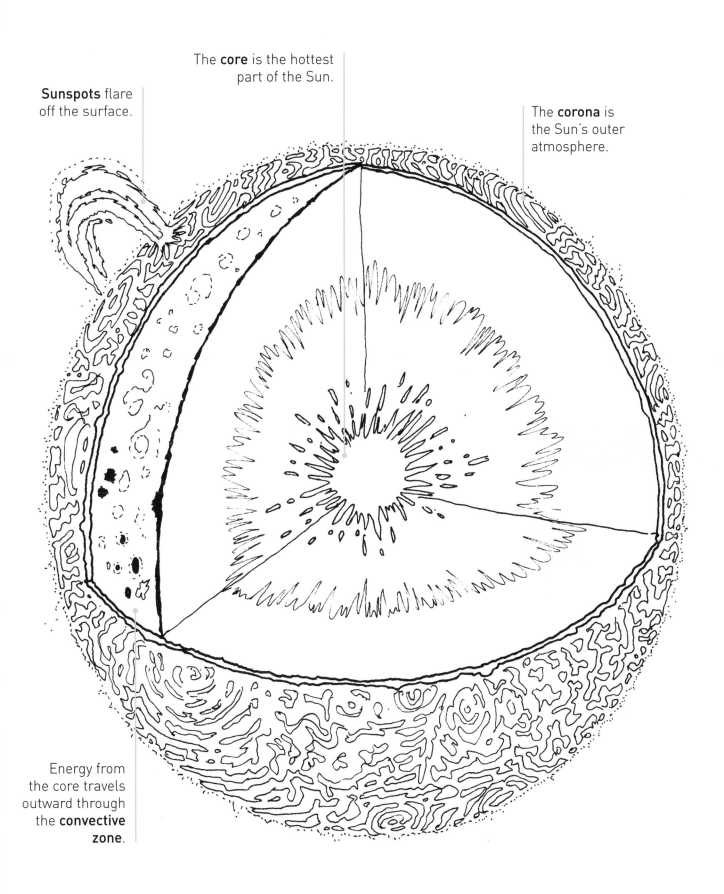

The **core** is the hottest part of the Sun.

**Sunspots** flare off the surface.

The **corona** is the Sun's outer atmosphere.

Energy from the core travels outward through the **convective zone**.

# SUNSPOTS AND SOLAR FLARES

Sunspots are darker areas that can be seen on the surface of the Sun if projected onto a piece of card through a telescope.

Solar flares are massive explosions that shoot matter out into space. The solar wind is made up of particles that are constantly being given off by the Sun, and is strongest when the sunspot activity is at its height.

## QUICK FACTS

Many sunspots leap up, along, and down in a curved **ARC** back to the Sun. The largest ones can be more than 300,000 miles long.

Sunspots usually vary in an **11-YEAR CYCLE**. An average sunspot's "life" is two weeks.

The **LARGEST** sunspot seen so far, covering more than 13 times the area of Earth, happened on March 30 2001.

If solar flares head toward the Earth, they can affect radio and television signals, and can cause **AURORAS** as they bump into the Earth's magnetic field.

One huge solar flare in 1989 caused a **POWER CUT** in Canada that left six million people without electricity.

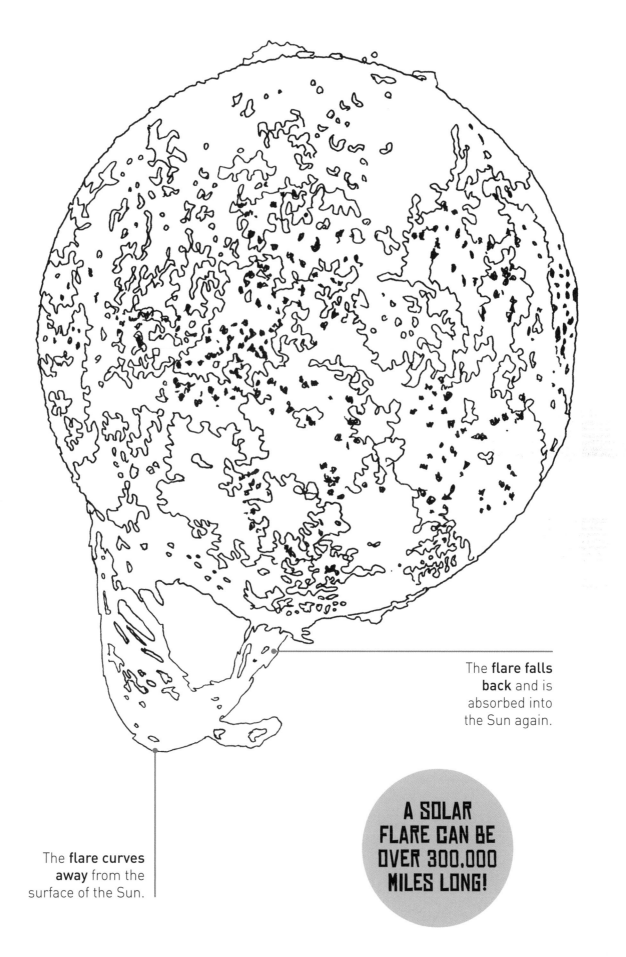

The **flare falls back** and is absorbed into the Sun again.

The **flare curves away** from the surface of the Sun.

A SOLAR FLARE CAN BE OVER 300,000 MILES LONG!

# THE PLANETS

Our Earth is just one of eight planets in the Solar System.

The dotted lines represent the way every planet **orbits** the Sun.

**Mars** is the closest planet to Earth.

**Earth** is our home.

The **asteroid belt** consists of millions of rocks.

**Venus** is the hottest planet.

**Mercury** is tiny and barren.

**Jupiter** is the biggest planet.

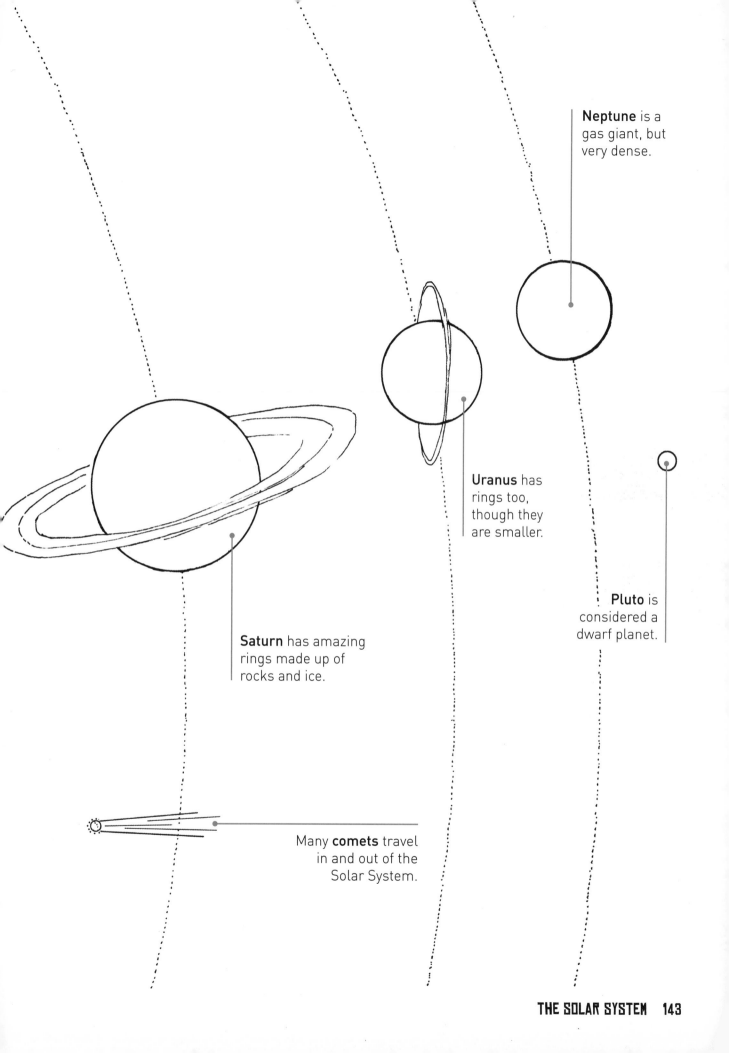

**Neptune** is a gas giant, but very dense.

**Uranus** has rings too, though they are smaller.

**Pluto** is considered a dwarf planet.

**Saturn** has amazing rings made up of rocks and ice.

Many **comets** travel in and out of the Solar System.

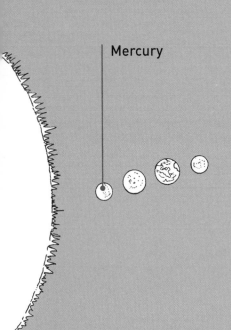

Mercury

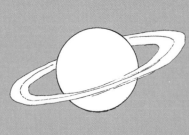

# MERCURY

Mercury is the closest planet to the Sun, meaning that it is blasted by solar heat and other radiation. This has swept away all but the flimsiest atmosphere, and heats Mercury's daytime side to incredible temperatures, yet the night side plunges into darkness and cold.

It has several hundred craters named after famous artists and classical musicians, such as Dickens, Shakespeare, Chopin, Mark Twain, and Beethoven.

## QUICK FACTS

The best-known feature on Mercury is the Caloris Basin, a massive **CRATER** measuring 840 miles across.

------

Mercury was known in **ANCIENT TIMES** because of its brief periods of visibility at dawn and dusk.

------

It is named after the **ROMAN** messenger of the gods.

------

The planet **ORBITS** the Sun at an average speed of 29.8 miles per second.

------

Between 2011 and 2013, NASA's *Messenger* spacecraft **MAPPED** the entire planet for the first time in history.

------

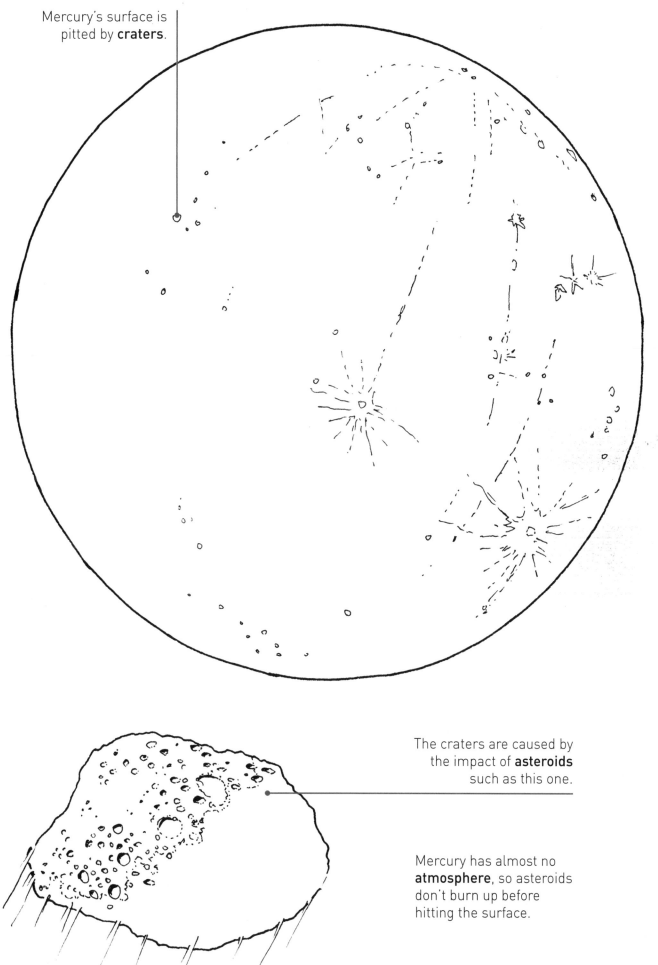

Mercury's surface is pitted by **craters**.

The craters are caused by the impact of **asteroids** such as this one.

Mercury has almost no **atmosphere**, so asteroids don't burn up before hitting the surface.

Venus

# VENUS

Although Venus is about the same size and mass (weight) as Earth, it could not be more different. It is the hottest of all the planets, partly because its thick atmosphere traps vast amounts of heat from the nearby Sun.

The temperature on the surface of the planet is nearly 930°F. It is shrouded by thick swirling clouds of gases, and droplets of acid that hide its surface from the gaze of outsiders.

## QUICK FACTS

Venus has at least 160 **VOLCANOES** that are larger than 62 miles in diameter, and over 50,000 smaller ones.

However, the volcanoes all appear to be **DEAD**.

Venus features the huge **MOUNTAINS** of the Ishtar Terra. These highlands are about the size of Australia.

Several **PROBES** have been sent to Venus, and radio waves have been used to map virtually the entire planet.

Because Venus was a Roman **GODDESS**, astronomers have named many of its features after famous women.

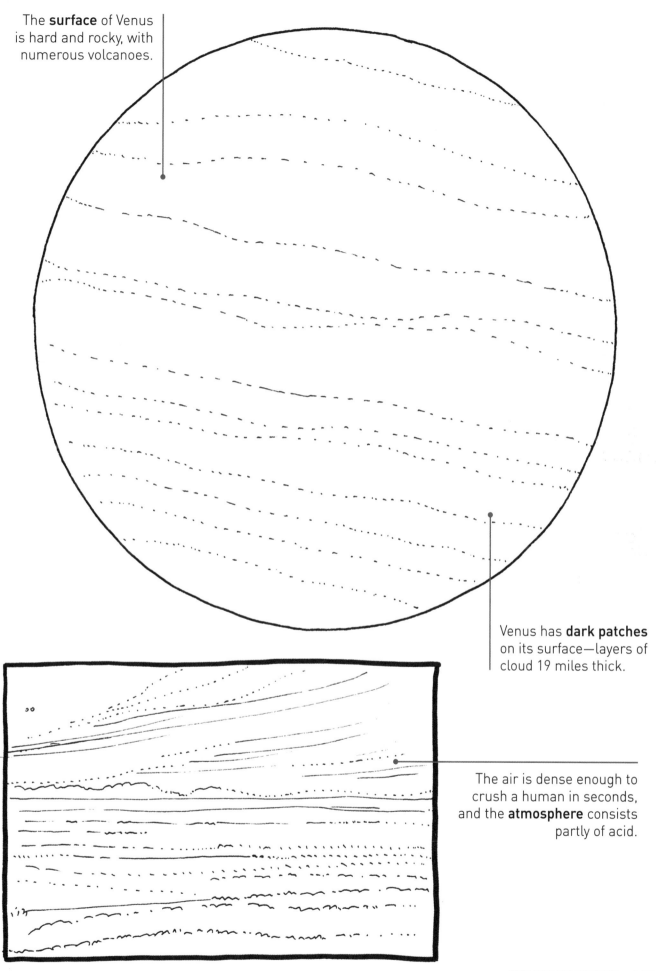

The **surface** of Venus is hard and rocky, with numerous volcanoes.

Venus has **dark patches** on its surface—layers of cloud 19 miles thick.

The air is dense enough to crush a human in seconds, and the **atmosphere** consists partly of acid.

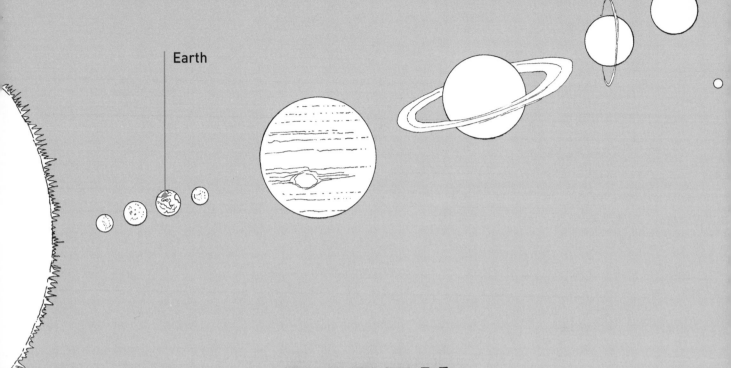

Earth

# EARTH

Our Earth is the third planet out from the Sun. Its single most outstanding feature is that it is the only place in the Universe known to maintain life.

People who have gone into space have come back with a changed perspective and reverence for the planet Earth. One astronaut said after his trip, "My first view—a panorama of brilliant deep blue ocean, shot with shades of green and gray and white—was of atolls and clouds."

## QUICK FACTS

Earth began to be **FORMED** over 4.5 billion years ago, but for millions of years nothing could live here.

Earth has two **MOTIONS**—it spins on its axis, and it moves in an orbit around the Sun.

In digging **MINES**, it has been found that the deeper the hole is made, the higher the temperature becomes.

At the **CORE**, the temperature is believed to be as high as 10,000°F.

The surface of the Earth is always changing. Over millions of years, an original, single land mass broke up and moved to become the **continents**.

Earth is surrounded by a thick blanket of air, called the **atmosphere**, which is made up of about 20 gases.

Beneath the land and water lie layers of **rock** and **metal** at very high temperatures.

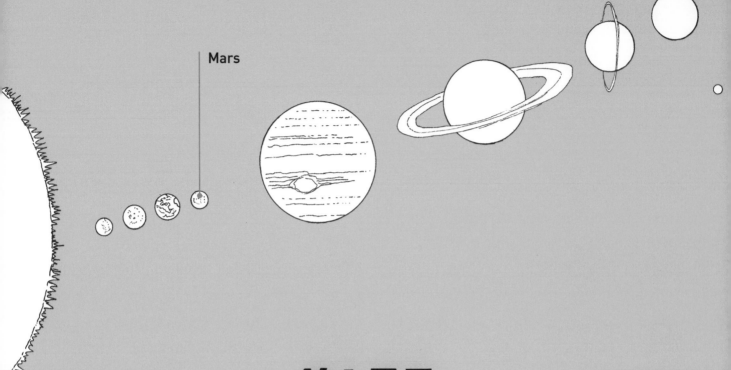

Mars

# MARS

Named after the Roman god of war, Mars is called the "Red Planet" because its surface rocks and dust contain large amounts of iron oxide—better known here on Earth as rust.

Mars shares many features with Earth, including volcanoes, canyons, winds, and swirling dust storms.

## QUICK FACTS

Astronomers believe that there was a great deal of liquid **WATER** on Mars billions of years ago.

Scientists have identified several **CHANNELS** that could only have been formed by running water.

However, like Earth, Mars has polar **ICE CAPS** made of water ice that remains through summer.

Nowadays, Mars has virtually no **ATMOSPHERE**.

Humans have always wondered if **MARTIANS** inhabit the Red Planet, yet despite many visits by space probes, landers, and rovers, no signs of life have been found.

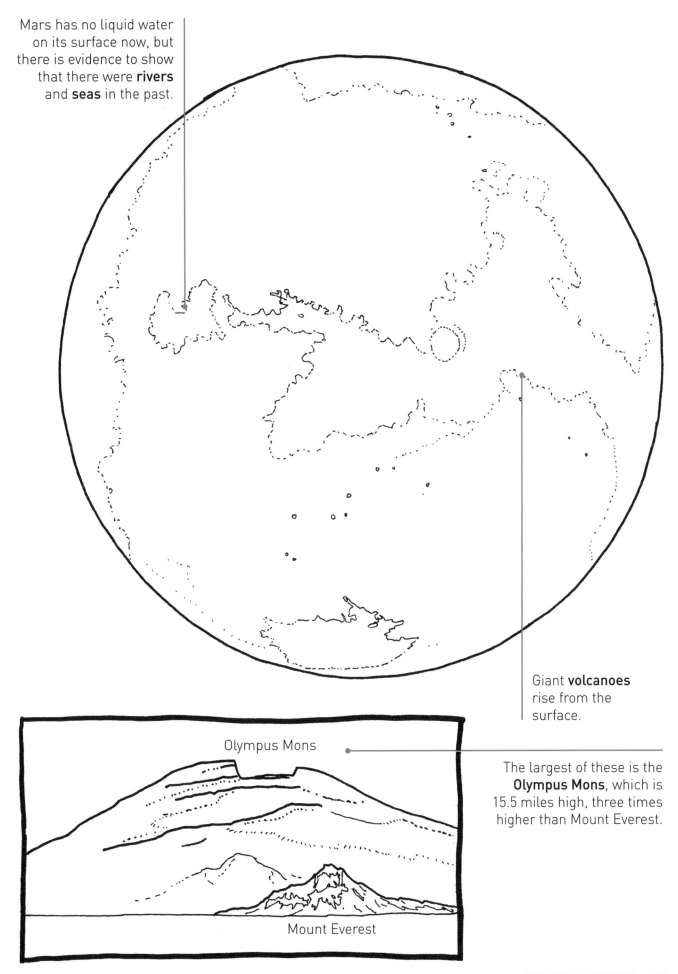

Mars has no liquid water on its surface now, but there is evidence to show that there were **rivers** and **seas** in the past.

Giant **volcanoes** rise from the surface.

Olympus Mons

Mount Everest

The largest of these is the **Olympus Mons**, which is 15.5 miles high, three times higher than Mount Everest.

Jupiter

# JUPITER

By far the biggest planet in the Solar System is Jupiter—a
vast world of swirling gases, and storms of unimaginable fury.
It is the fifth planet from the Sun in terms of distance,
but is also, the nearest "gas giant" to the Sun.

It has more than twice as much mass than all the
other eight planets added together.

## QUICK FACTS

Jupiter is not much smaller than some of the smallest
**STARS**, but it does not shine itself, and reflects sunlight
as all planets do.

Its huge pull of gravity holds more than 60 **MOONS** in
orbit around it.

Jupiter is named after the Roman **KING OF THE GODS**.

Jupiter is not only the largest planet, it also **SPINS**
around the fastest: once in fewer than 10 Earth hours.

The spinning **SPEED** of the upper atmosphere at the
equator is five minutes faster than at the poles, so the
atmosphere is continually being twisted and torn.

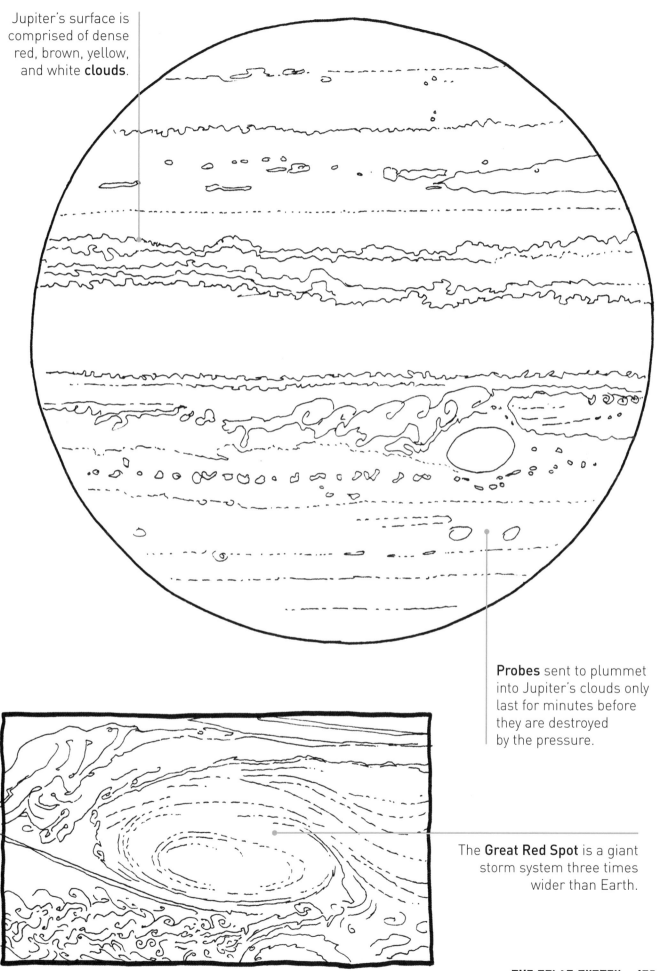

Jupiter's surface is comprised of dense red, brown, yellow, and white **clouds**.

**Probes** sent to plummet into Jupiter's clouds only last for minutes before they are destroyed by the pressure.

The **Great Red Spot** is a giant storm system three times wider than Earth.

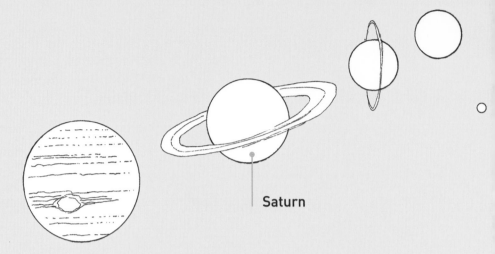

Saturn

# SATURN

Saturn, the second-largest planet after neighboring Jupiter, is perhaps the planet best-known for having rings around it. They are only 328 ft thick, but they extend into space for 47 miles.

Saturn is the only planet whose density, or mass per volume, is less than water. If there was a tank of water big enough, Saturn could float!

## QUICK FACTS

Saturn is a **GAS GIANT**, like Jupiter, but smaller.

The material in the rings was probably captured by Saturn's **GRAVITY** when the Solar System was forming.

Another theory is that it might be the remains of a shattered **MOON**.

Some of the rings are **BRAIDED** or twisted.

The rings of Saturn were first noticed by Galileo, who could not quite make them out with his early telescope. He guessed they might be moons, one on each side, and called them the "**EARS**" of Saturn.

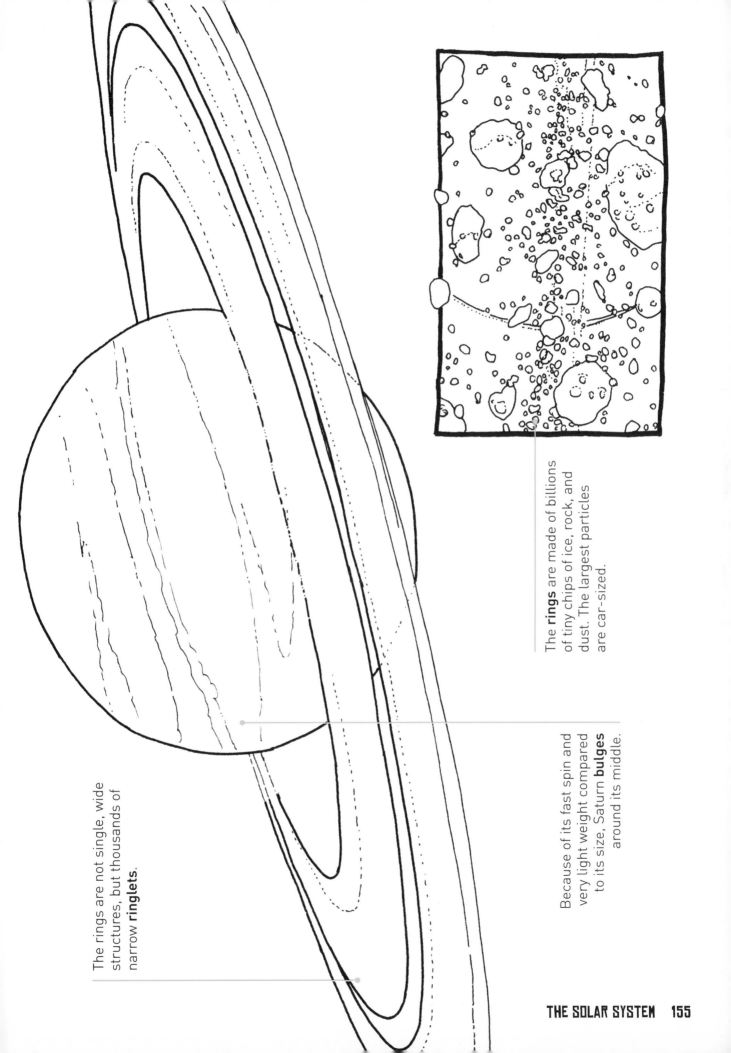

The **rings** are made of billions of tiny chips of ice, rock, and dust. The largest particles are car-sized.

The rings are not single, wide structures, but thousands of narrow **ringlets**.

Because of its fast spin and very light weight compared to its size, Saturn **bulges** around its middle.

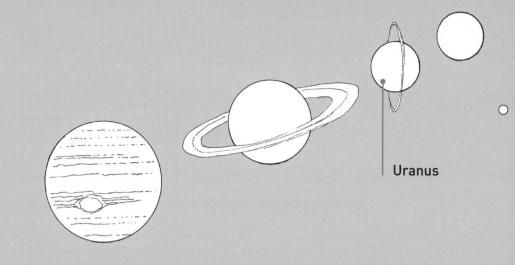

Uranus

# URANUS

Uranus is a gas giant, but smaller than both Jupiter and Saturn.

It was the first planet to be found with the aid of a telescope. It was discovered in 1781 by astronomer William Herschel, who originally thought it was a comet or a star.

## QUICK FACTS

Although Saturn is the planet everyone thinks of when it comes to having **RINGS**, Jupiter, Neptune, and Uranus have them too.

A **DAY** on Uranus lasts 17 hours and 40 minutes in Earth time.

The planet is named after the ancient Greek deity of the heavens, the earliest supreme god.

Uranus has been visited by only one spacecraft, *Voyager 2*, in January 1986.

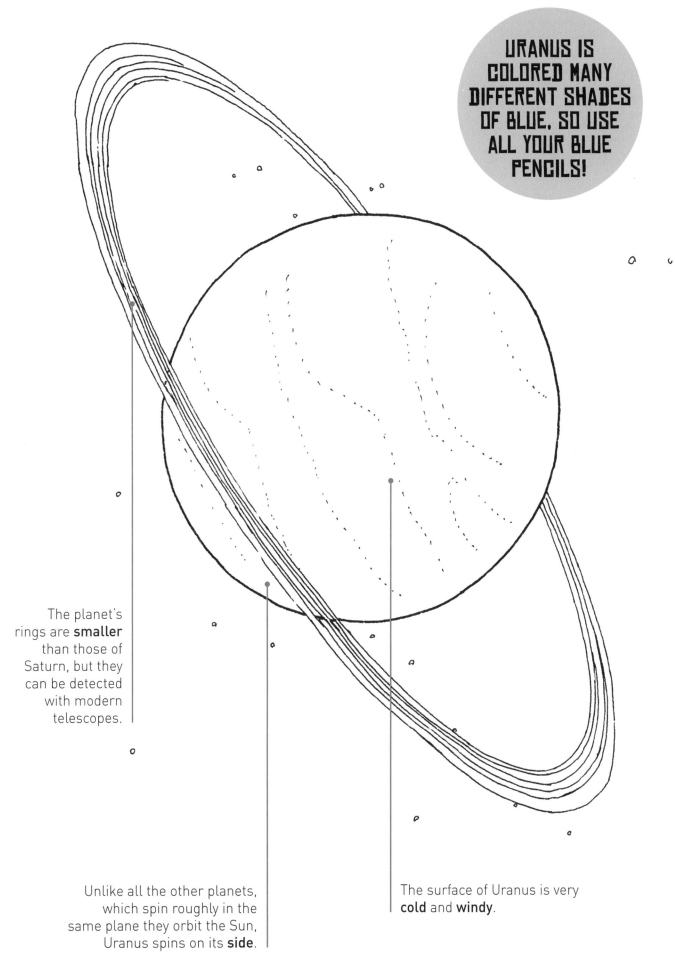

The planet's rings are **smaller** than those of Saturn, but they can be detected with modern telescopes.

Unlike all the other planets, which spin roughly in the same plane they orbit the Sun, Uranus spins on its **side**.

The surface of Uranus is very **cold** and **windy**.

Neptune

# NEPTUNE

Neptune is the most distant planet in the Solar
System, and we know little about it.

It is a very cold place. At the farthest part of its orbit it is 2,485 million miles
from the Sun, and its surface temperature can drop as low as –346°F.

## QUICK FACTS

Neptune was found in **1846** when astronomers
determined that an unknown planet was disturbing
the orbit of Uranus.

Neptune has huge storms, and one of these,
the **GREAT DARK SPOT**, was larger than Earth.

The Great Dark Spot was first **SEEN** in 1989,
and by 1994 it had gone.

Neptune takes an **AMAZING** 164.8 years to travel once
around the Sun.

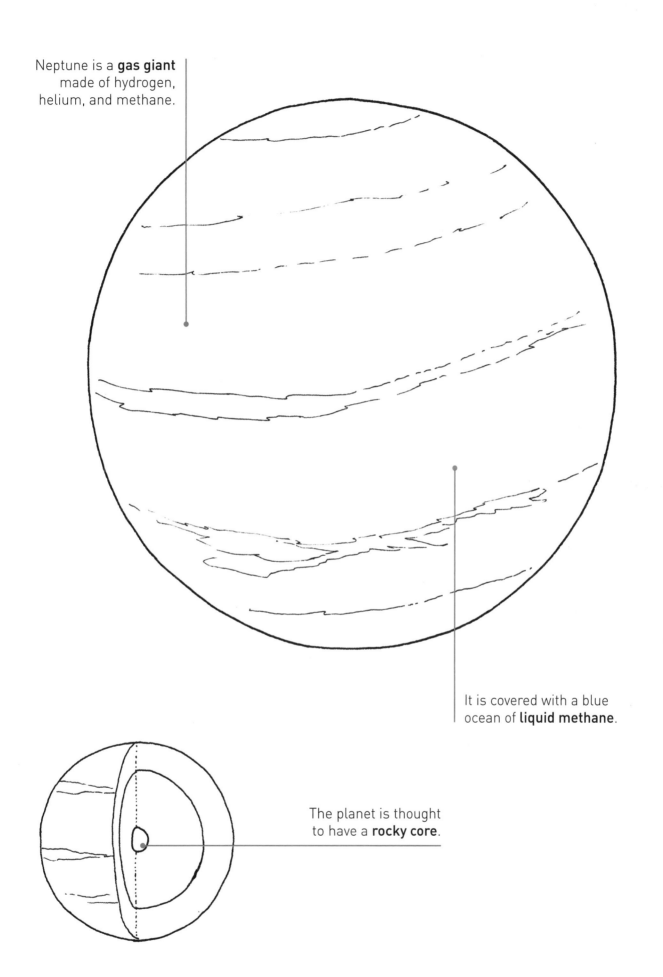

Neptune is a **gas giant** made of hydrogen, helium, and methane.

It is covered with a blue ocean of **liquid methane**.

The planet is thought to have a **rocky core**.

Pluto

# PLUTO

Pluto is part of the Kuiper Belt, a region on the edge of the Solar System containing many comet-like objects.

It is always dark and cold on Pluto, even in the middle of the day. This is because the Sun appears 1,000 times fainter from the surface of Pluto than it does from Earth: little more than a faint star.

## QUICK FACTS

Pluto was only **DISCOVERED** in 1930. Astronomers noticed that Neptune's orbit was being disturbed by an unknown object, which turned out to be Pluto.

Initially Pluto was **CLASSIFIED** as a planet.

However, it is now considered to be a **DWARF PLANET** rather than a true planet.

Pluto's **ATMOSPHERE** probably consists primarily of nitrogen with some carbon monoxide and methane.

If all the objects in the **KUIPER BELT** joined together, they would form a planet the size of Earth.

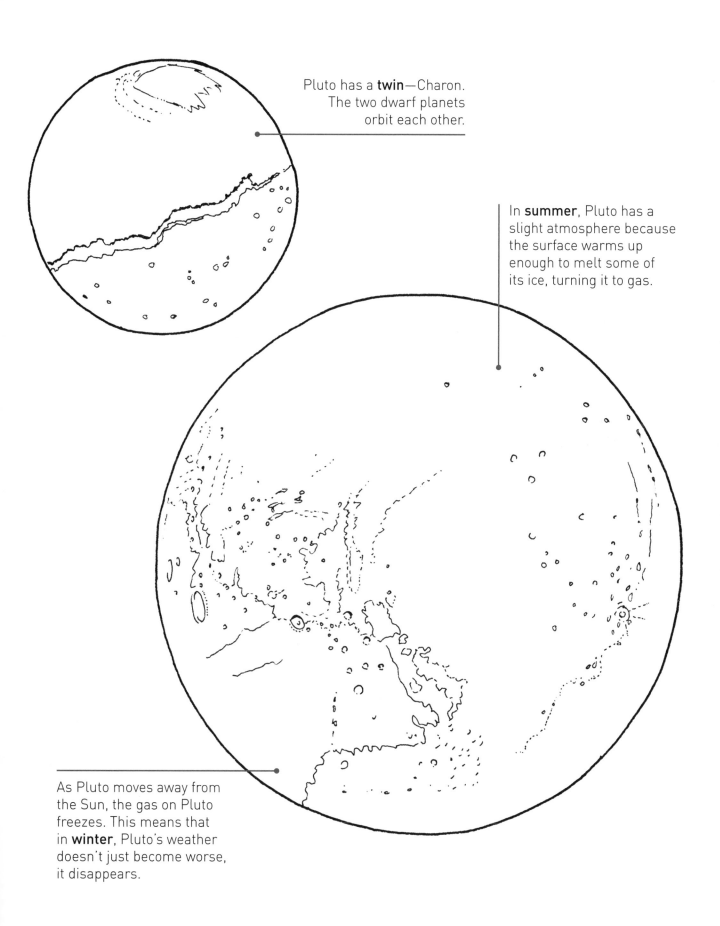

Pluto has a **twin**—Charon. The two dwarf planets orbit each other.

In **summer**, Pluto has a slight atmosphere because the surface warms up enough to melt some of its ice, turning it to gas.

As Pluto moves away from the Sun, the gas on Pluto freezes. This means that in **winter**, Pluto's weather doesn't just become worse, it disappears.

# OUR MOON

A moon is a natural object of reasonable size going around a planet. The one we call the Moon (usually with "the" and a capital "M") is Earth's single moon. It has its own faint atmosphere, containing helium, neon, hydrogen, and argon.

Seen from Earth, the Moon is about the same size as the Sun.

## QUICK FACTS

**DAY** and **NIGHT** on the Moon are not the same length as on the Earth: each lasts for roughly 14 days.

The average **DISTANCE** of the Moon from the Earth is 239,000 miles.

There are some huge valleys called **RILLES**, which can be hundreds of miles in length and look a little like riverbeds.

The average **TEMPERATURE** on the surface of the Moon is –9.4ºF. It can drop to –770.8ºF and rise to 22.5ºF.

It is thought the Moon was **FORMED** some 4,500 million years ago when a huge Mars-sized lump of rock crashed into Earth. The loose matter and debris orbiting Earth after the impact came together to form the Moon.

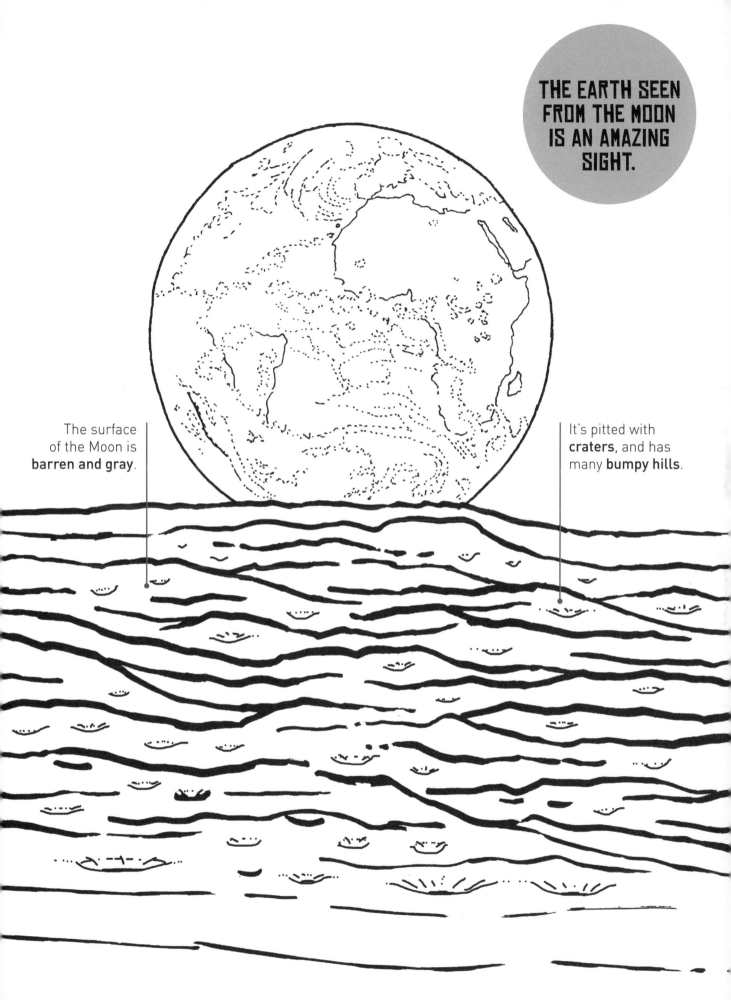

THE EARTH SEEN FROM THE MOON IS AN AMAZING SIGHT.

The surface of the Moon is **barren and gray**.

It's pitted with **craters**, and has many **bumpy hills**.

# WATCHING THE MOON

The Moon is by far the brightest object in the night sky, but it has no light of its own. Moonlight is simply the reflected light of the Sun. Parts of the Moon that are not in sunlight are invisible against the deep blackness of space. Think of the Sun as a light bulb, and the Moon as a mirror, reflecting light from the light bulb.

## QUICK FACTS

The Moon **TURNS AROUND** once in the same time it takes to go around Earth once. This means that it keeps mainly one side facing Earth.

Most of its **CRATERS** are named after famous scientists.

The **FAR SIDE** of the Moon was a mystery until 1959, when a Russian space probe took the first photographs of it.

The actual appearance of the far side was something of a **DISAPPOINTMENT**, because it had far fewer craters than the familiar side that always faces Earth.

**MOUNTAIN RANGES**, thousands of feet high, form the walls of huge craters on the Moon's surface.

Sometimes the Moon seems to **change color**. This mostly happens when there is a lot of dust, smoke, or pollution in the atmosphere. The size of those particles will determine what you see.

Sometimes it looks **red**...

...orange...

...or even **blue**.

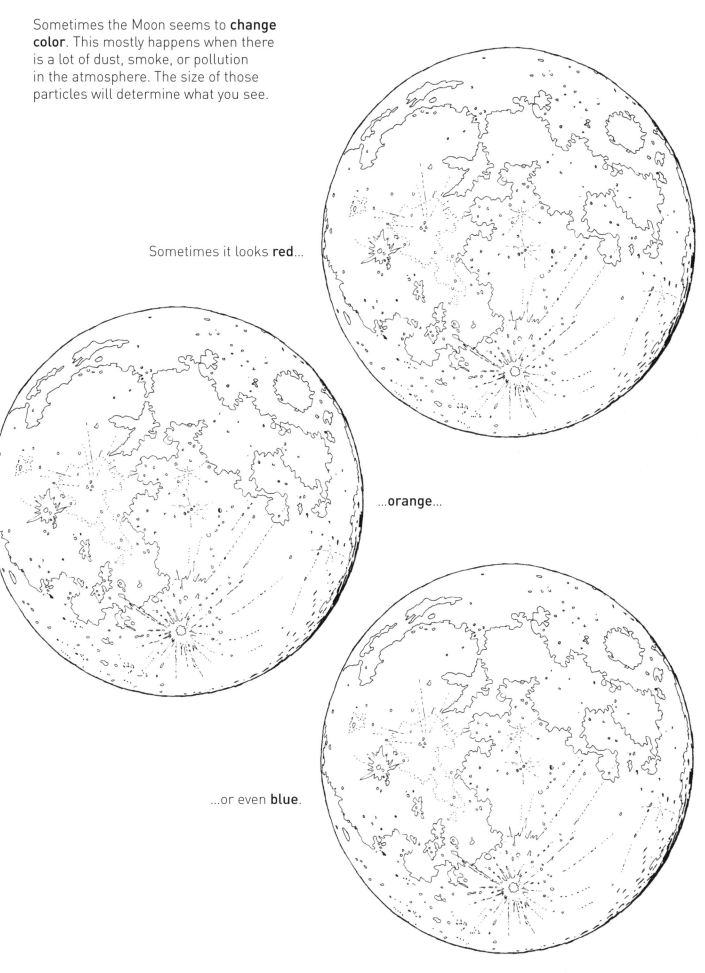

# MOONS OF THE PLANETS

Most of the planets in our Solar System have moons. They are natural satellites, and many dozens of such objects have so far been discovered. Jupiter has the most, with over 60 confirmed.

Natural satellites vary greatly in size. Some of them measure only a few miles in diameter, as in the case of the two tiny moons of Mars and the outer satellites of Jupiter.

## QUICK FACTS

Mercury and Venus are the only two planets in the Solar System that have **NO MOONS**.

Earth only has **ONE MOON**, which is unusual. Some of the larger planets have many each.

Most moons are heavily **CRATERED**, from asteroid strikes.

**GANYMEDE**, one of the satellites of Jupiter, is the largest moon in the Solar System. It was discovered by the Italian astronomer Galileo Galilei in 1610.

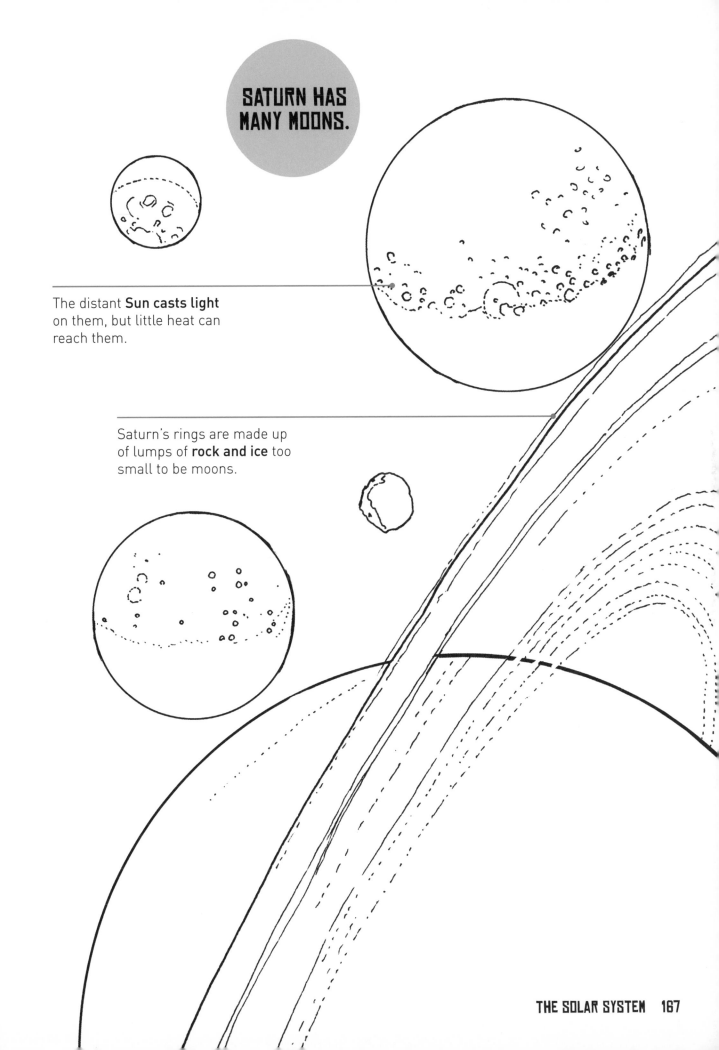

**SATURN HAS MANY MOONS.**

The distant **Sun casts light** on them, but little heat can reach them.

Saturn's rings are made up of lumps of **rock and ice** too small to be moons.

# MOONS OF JUPITER

Some of the moons orbiting the giant planet Jupiter are as large as Mercury, and bigger than the dwarf planet Pluto. Callisto, Io, and Europa are all very different. The surface of Europa is made of ice, and scientists even think that the oceans on Europa could provide a home for living things, under their thick surface layer of ice.

## QUICK FACTS

**IO** is the most geologically active (volcanic) object in the Solar System.

---

The biggest asteroid impacts on **CALLISTO** have cracked the surface to form huge bullseye patterns.

---

Callisto's **SURFACE** is blanketed by dark dirt that gathered when icy crater rims and cliffs crumbled away.

---

Europa's interior is hotter than its surface. This internal heat comes from the **GRAVITATIONAL** forces of Jupiter and Jupiter's other large satellites, which pull Europa in different directions.

---

**EUROPA** is one of the smoothest objects in the Solar System. Its surface features include shallow cracks, valleys, ridges, pits, blisters, and icy flows.

---

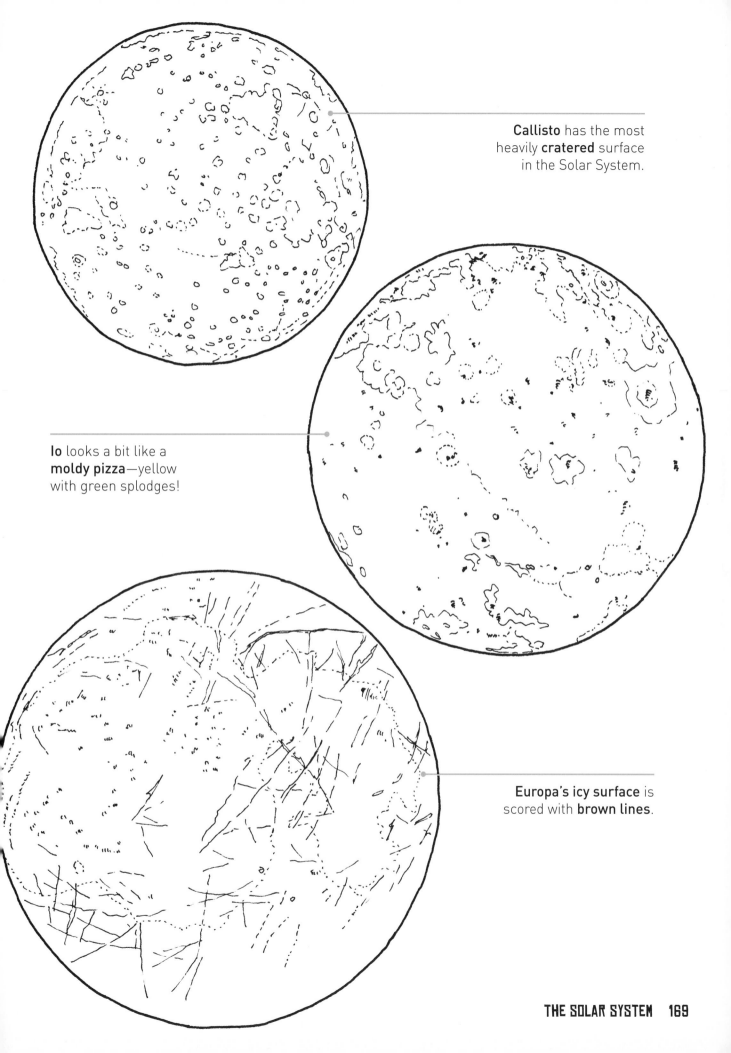

Callisto has the most heavily **cratered** surface in the Solar System.

**Io** looks a bit like a **moldy pizza**—yellow with green splodges!

Europa's icy surface is scored with **brown lines**.

# THE NORTHERN LIGHTS

Where solar wind interacts with Earth's magnetic fields, near the North and South Poles, it creates an aurora.

These shimmering "curtains" of light high in the sky are called the Northern Lights (the aurora borealis) and Southern Lights (the aurora australis).

## QUICK FACTS

Some ancient cultures thought that the Northern Lights were celestial dancers, or the **SOULS** of dead warriors.

The **TILT** of the Earth causes northern countries to get more of the Sun's light.

In northern **SCANDINAVIA** it doesn't get dark at all in the middle of summer.

Another amazing sight in the sky is a **SOLAR ECLIPSE**. This happens for a brief period when the Moon, Earth, and Sun are in line. The Moon blocks the Sun's light.

A **LUNAR ECLIPSE** happens when the Earth lies between the Moon and the Sun, blocking off the light to the Moon, so that the Moon seems to vanish.

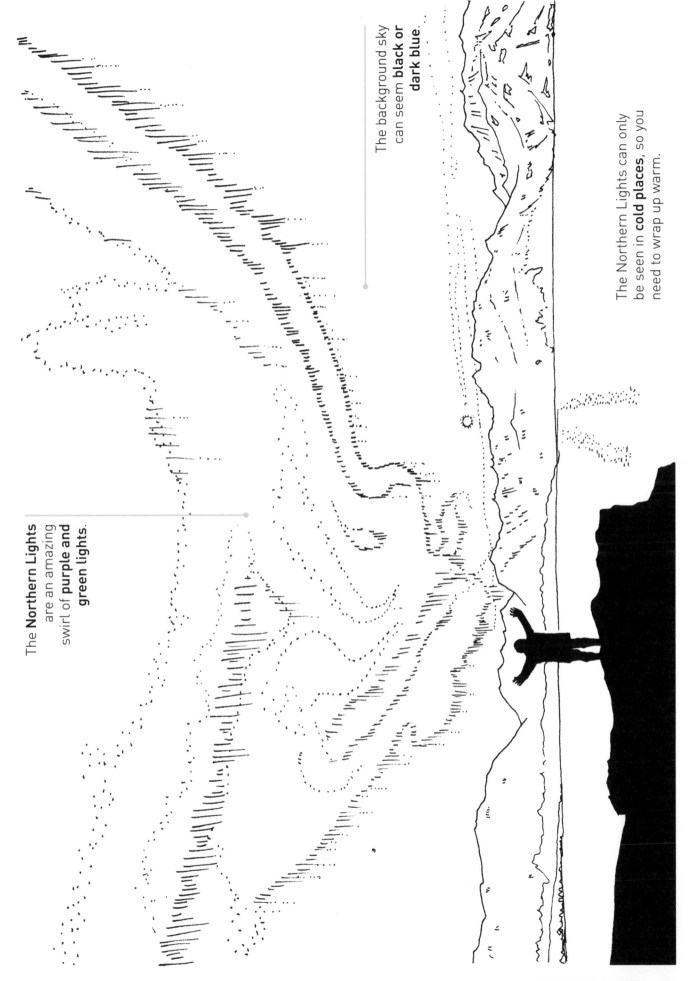

The **Northern Lights** are an amazing swirl of **purple and green lights**.

The background sky can seem **black or dark blue**.

The Northern Lights can only be seen in **cold places**, so you need to wrap up warm.

# ASTEROIDS

Asteroids are chunks of rock that orbit the Sun. They are pieces of rock left over from the formation of the planets and moons.

There is an asteroid "belt" in our Solar System, located between Mars and Jupiter. Scientists think the belt may have formed when a small planet shattered because of the pull of Jupiter's strong gravity.

## QUICK FACTS

Asteroids are sometimes known as **PLANETOIDS**, or minor planets.

Humans have identified and named more than **7,000** asteroids.

Asteroids **SPIN** as they fly through space.

The **BIGGEST-KNOWN** asteroid is Ceres, which is 580 miles across.

The asteroid Ida has a small **MOON** of its own, Dactyl.

Asteroids have hit Earth in the past. A major impact about 65 million years ago may be linked to the extinction of the **DINOSAURS**.

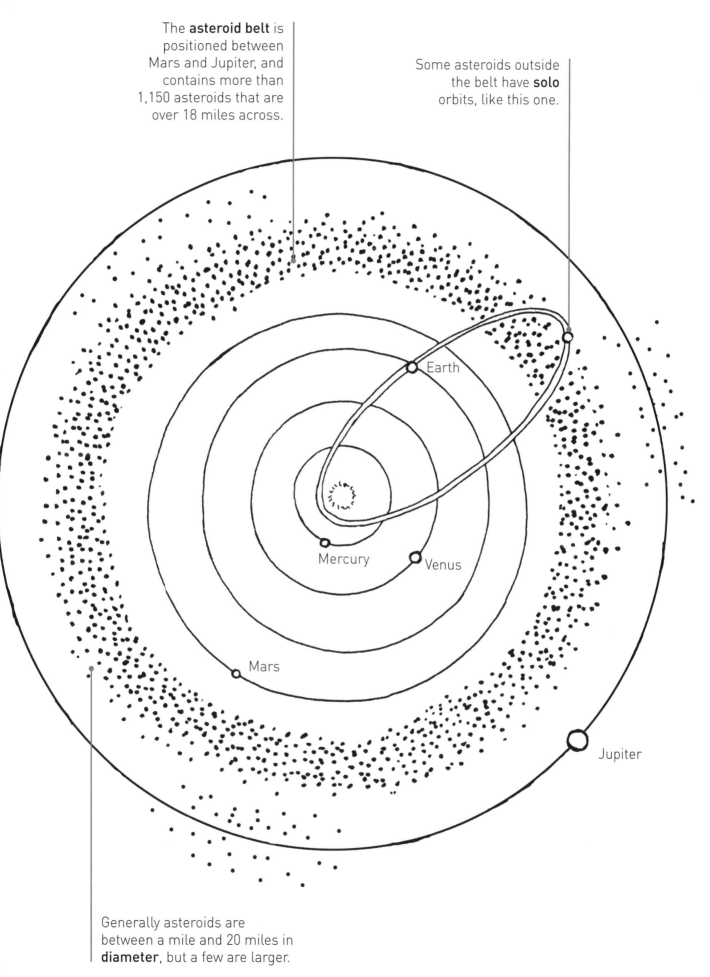

The **asteroid belt** is positioned between Mars and Jupiter, and contains more than 1,150 asteroids that are over 18 miles across.

Some asteroids outside the belt have **solo** orbits, like this one.

Earth

Mercury

Venus

Mars

Jupiter

Generally asteroids are between a mile and 20 miles in **diameter**, but a few are larger.

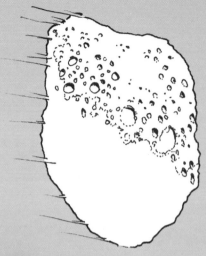

# METEORS

Look up into a clear sky at night, and you might be lucky enough to see a streak of light. It appears for only a fraction of a second and then it is gone.

The bright streak is called a meteor, and is made by a particle of dust entering Earth's atmosphere from space and burning up. Large meteors that survive their journey down through the atmosphere and hit the ground are called meteorites.

## QUICK FACTS

Meteorites enter Earth's **ATMOSPHERE** at speeds of at least seven miles per second, which makes them glow brightly.

**SEVERAL THOUSAND** meteorites enter Earth's atmosphere every year, but very few reach the ground.

The largest-known meteorite is made of iron, and weighs **72 TONS**. It probably fell to Earth in prehistoric times in what is now called Namibia.

When a large meteorite hits Earth, it releases energy equivalent to hundreds of **NUCLEAR BOMBS**.

The most brilliant **METEOR SHOWER** known took place in November 1833.

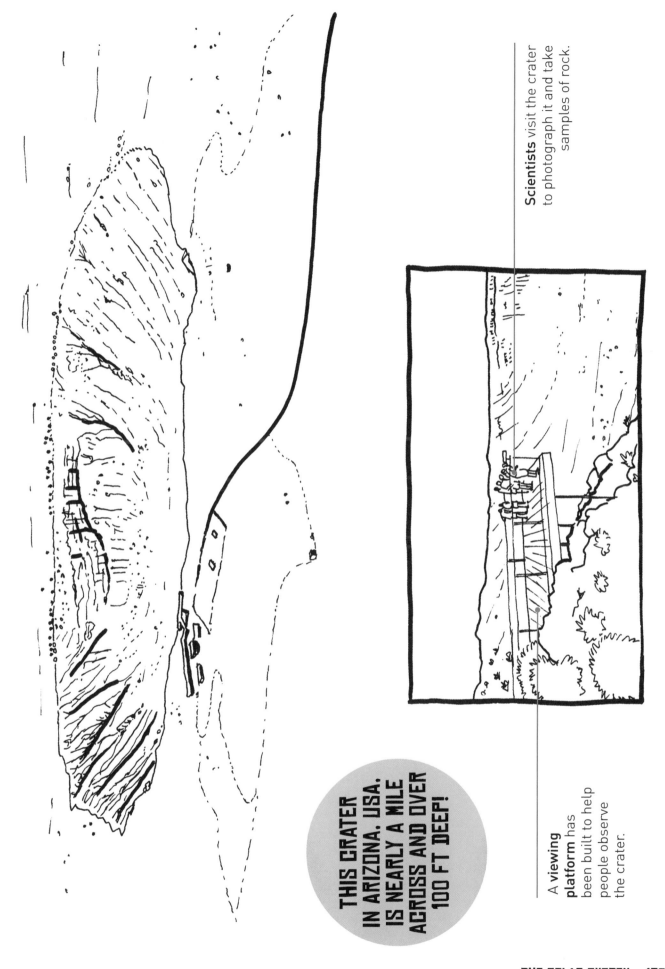

**THIS CRATER IN ARIZONA, USA, IS NEARLY A MILE ACROSS AND OVER 100 FT DEEP!**

**Scientists** visit the crater to photograph it and take samples of rock.

A **viewing platform** has been built to help people observe the crater.

# COMETS

Every few years, an object that looks like a fuzzy star with a long bright tail appears in the sky. These strange objects are not stars. They are comets.

A comet is a chunk of gas and dust and ice left over from the formation of the Solar System. Comets orbit the Sun. When a comet nears the Sun, some of the ice on its surface evaporates and releases dust, forming a tail.

Most comets are too dim to be seen with the naked eye, but every 10 years or so an especially bright one appears in the sky.

## QUICK FACTS

Comets are sometimes known as **DIRTY SNOWBALLS**.

A comet **TAIL** appears as a smear of light that moves very gradually across the sky.

**HALLEY'S COMET** is perhaps the most famous of all. It can be seen from Earth every 76 years, and was even recorded in 1066 on the Bayeux Tapestry. Its most recent visit to Earth was in 1986.

Comet tails are very different in shape and size. Some are short and **STUBBY**. Others are long and **SLENDER**.

If all the known comets were added together, they would **WEIGH** less than the Moon.

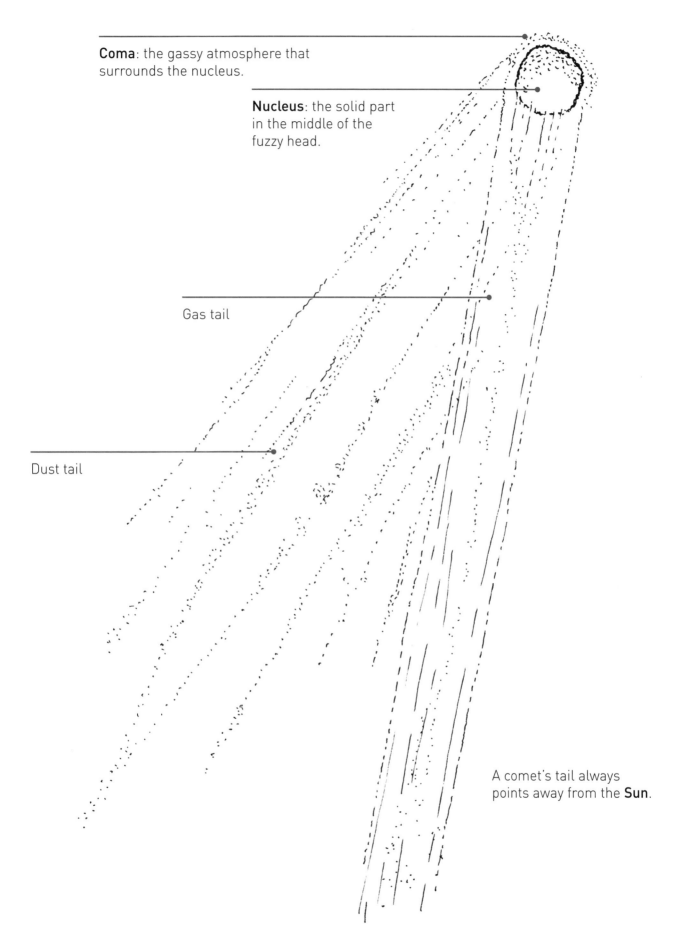

**Coma**: the gassy atmosphere that surrounds the nucleus.

**Nucleus**: the solid part in the middle of the fuzzy head.

Gas tail

Dust tail

A comet's tail always points away from the **Sun**.

# SPACE EXPLORATION

# EARLY ASTRONOMERS

The earliest astronomers were not interested in how the Universe worked. They needed to know when to plant or harvest crops and when rivers would flood, and they used the movements of bodies in the heavens to make calendars and to predict events in the future.

Consequently, at one stage, astrology and astronomy became intertwined. It was the ancient Greeks who first started to ask questions about the Universe and how it worked. Their work was built on by the studies of great European astronomers from the 15th century onward.

## QUICK FACTS

**2nd century BCE**: Hipparchus of Nicaea cataloged more than 800 stars, and calculated the length of Earth's **YEAR** to within 6.5 minutes.

**2nd century BCE**: Ptolemy of Alexandria devised a model of the Solar System with the Earth at the **CENTER** and the Sun, Moon, planets, and stars circling it.

**16th century CE**: Polish astronomer Copernicus realized that Earth and the other planets revolve around the **SUN**.

**17th century CE**: Danish astronomer Tycho Brahe discovered a **SUPERNOVA** and suggested that it was outside the Solar System.

**17th century CE**: German astronomer Johannes Kepler devised the laws of planetary motion, linking a planet's **ORBIT** and speed to the Sun.

Hipparchus

Ptolemy

Copernicus

Tycho Brahe

Johannes Kepler

# LATER ASTRONOMERS

After the telescope was invented, many more people began gazing up at the night sky. Some were hobbyists but they sometimes chanced upon an amazing discovery that put their name forever into the history books.

Others were full-time professional astronomers who spent a lifetime observing and recording, yet their names are known to very few. This element of chance is smaller today, but it still exists, and draws millions of people to watch the skies every night.

## QUICK FACTS

**17th century CE**: Italian astronomer Galileo Galilei began using a telescope. He saw mountains and craters on the **MOON**, and discovered four moons orbiting Jupiter.

---

**17th century CE**: British astronomer John Flamsteed made the first extensive **STAR CHARTS** as part of work aimed at giving sailors a better method of navigation.

---

**17th–18th century CE**: British astronomer Edmund Halley discovered the **COMET** that is named after him.

---

**20th century CE**: American astronomer Edwin Hubble determined that there are other **GALAXIES** outside the Milky Way.

---

**21st century CE**: British scientist Stephen Hawking is working on a **THEORY** that could unite the four basic forces in the universe: gravity, electromagnetism, strong nuclear, and weak nuclear forces.

---

Galileo Galilei

John Flamsteed

Edmund Halley

Edwin Hubble

Stephen Hawking

# SPACE PROBES

Space probes are small packages of instruments that are launched from Earth to explore planets.

The world's first artificial satellite was *Sputnik 1* on October 4 1957. Since that time, probes have explored the surface of Mars, created maps of Venus and Mercury, taken close-up photographs of nearly all the planets and many of their moons, orbited Saturn, and even left the Solar System altogether.

## QUICK FACTS

**1966**: *Luna 9* lands on the **MOON**, and sends back the first close-up images of the Moon's surface.

**1970**: *Venera 7* makes the first successful landing on **VENUS**.

**1992**: The probe *Ulysses* is launched to study the Sun's north and south poles, and **SOLAR** wind.

**1994**: Parts of **COMET** Shoemaker-Levy 9 hit Jupiter in July, and are photographed by the approaching *Galileo* space probe.

**1997**: *Voyager 1* and *Voyager 2* are launched to study the **OUTER PLANETS**. These probes will later travel right outside our Solar System.

**2000**: The *Cassini* probe photographs **SATURN**.

**2015**: The *New Horizons* probe photographs **PLUTO**.

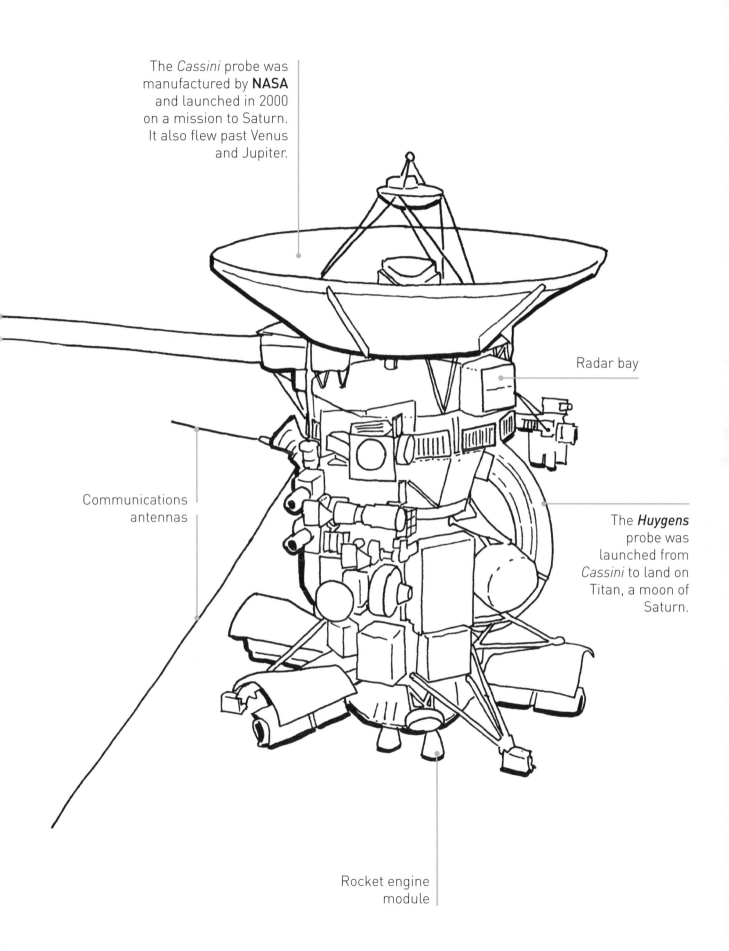

The *Cassini* probe was manufactured by **NASA** and launched in 2000 on a mission to Saturn. It also flew past Venus and Jupiter.

Radar bay

Communications antennas

The *Huygens* probe was launched from *Cassini* to land on Titan, a moon of Saturn.

Rocket engine module

# THE FIRST HUMAN IN SPACE

The first cosmonaut (the Russian word for astronaut) was the Russian Yuri Gagarin, who made the first-ever manned spaceflight on April 12 1961.

The flight lasted less than two hours from launch to landing.

## QUICK FACTS

Gagarin's *Vostok* **CAPSULE** was only big enough for one person. It was a sphere 8 ft across.

"Vostok" is Russian for "**EAST**".

On the way back down to Earth, Gagarin was ejected from his capsule at a height of 23,000 ft, and landed by **PARACHUTE**.

A **DOG** called Laika became the first living creature in space when the Russian satellite *Sputnik 2* carried her into orbit on November 3 1957.

Russian Valentina Tereshkova became the first **WOMAN** in space, on June 16 1963.

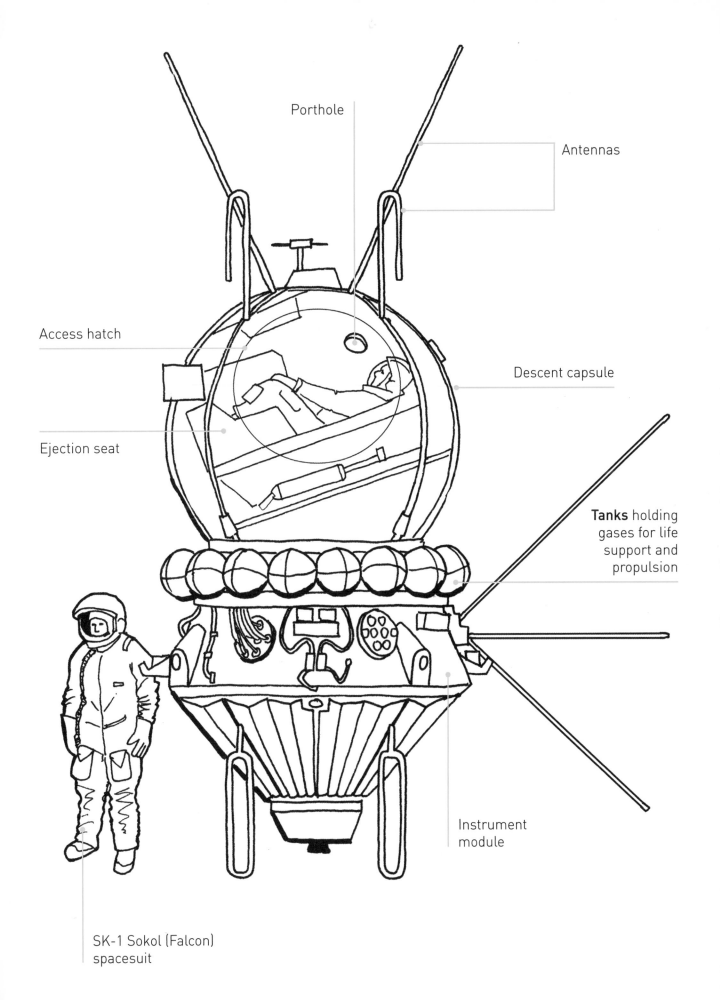

Porthole

Antennas

Access hatch

Descent capsule

Ejection seat

**Tanks** holding gases for life support and propulsion

Instrument module

SK-1 Sokol (Falcon) spacesuit

# THE FIRST HUMANS ON THE MOON

Neil Armstrong and Buzz Aldrin were the first men to land on the Moon's surface, in 1969, while Michael Collins circled the Moon in the *Apollo 11* Command Module.

## QUICK FACTS

The *Apollo* spacecraft were made of three **MODULES**: the Command Module, the Service Module, and the Lunar Excursion Module (LEM).

The **FOOTPRINTS** left by the astronauts will last for centuries because there is no wind on the Moon.

The **FLAG** the Americans left on the Moon is held out by a metal bar because there is no wind to make it fly.

In the last three *Apollo* missions, astronauts took the Lunar Roving Vehicle. This enabled them to **EXPLORE** further than had been possible before.

**NOBODY** has visited the Moon since 1972.

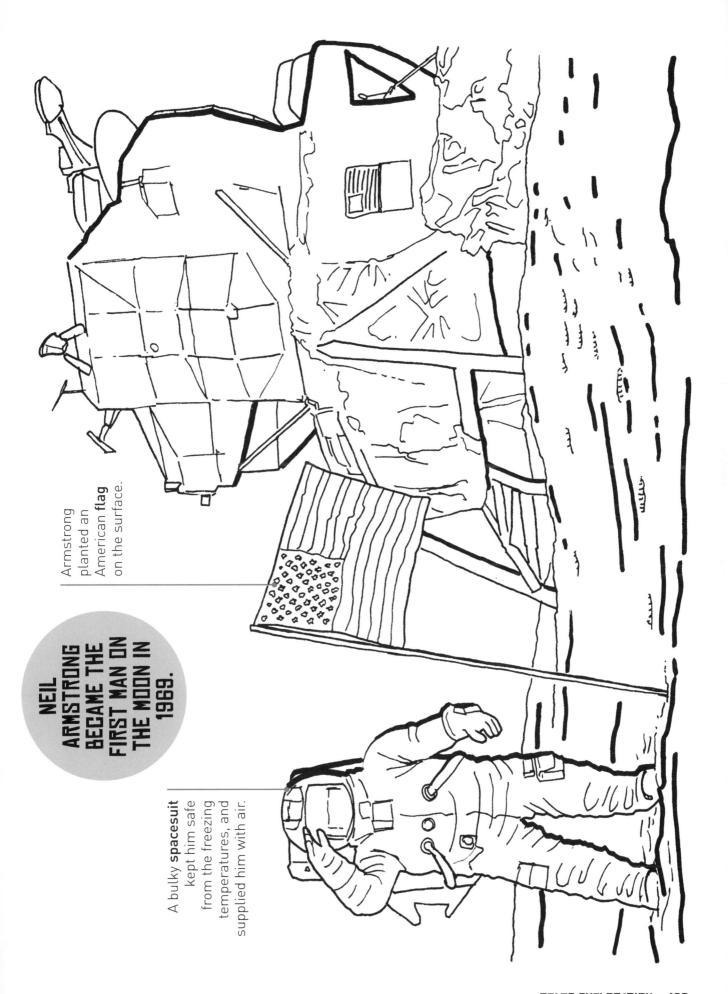

Armstrong planted an American **flag** on the surface.

NEIL ARMSTRONG BECAME THE FIRST MAN ON THE MOON IN 1969.

A bulky **spacesuit** kept him safe from the freezing temperatures, and supplied him with air.

# SPACE TELESCOPES

Observatories on Earth use two kinds of optical telescopes: reflecting telescopes and refracting telescopes. Reflecting telescopes use a set of such mirrors to focus light, and refracting telescopes use a system of lenses.

The atmosphere is constantly moving, which causes starlight to jiggle about as it passes through the air, and so stars appear to twinkle. Orbiting telescopes can view the skies without looking through the Earth's atmosphere.

## QUICK FACTS

The **HUBBLE** Space Telescope is a powerful telescope orbiting 380 miles above Earth. It provides sharper images than any other space telescope.

The Hubble telescope was built by the North American and European space agencies, and launched in 1990.

The refracting telescope at the Yerkes Observatory in Wisconsin, USA, has the world's largest lens.

Two identical telescopes called **KECK I** and **KECK II**, in Mauna Kea, Hawaii, USA, are the largest reflecting telescopes in the world.

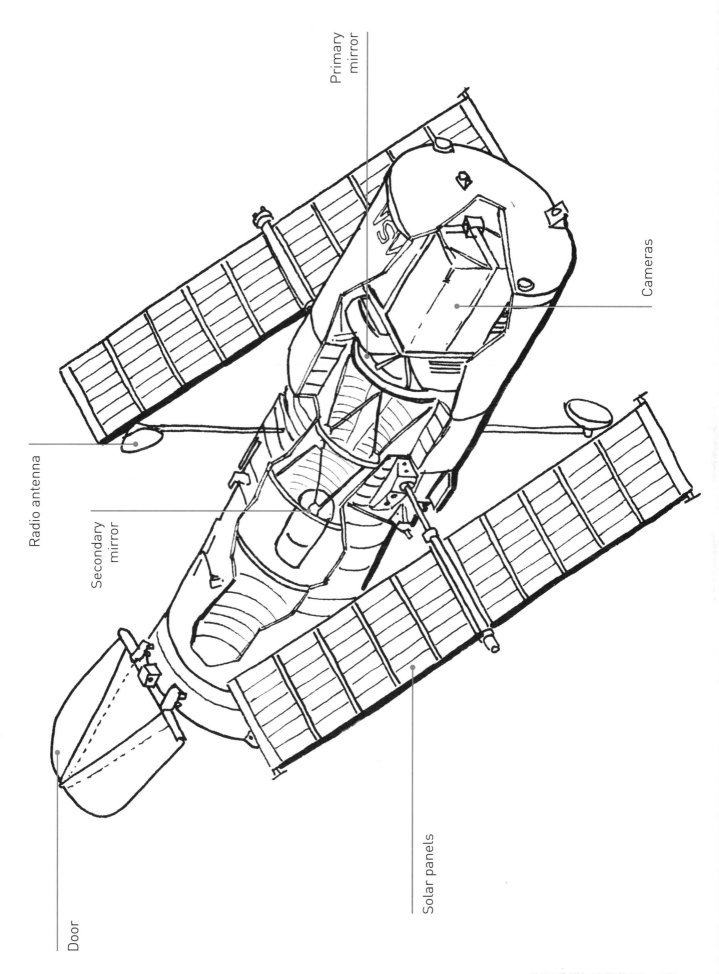

Primary mirror

Cameras

Radio antenna

Secondary mirror

Solar panels

Door

# THE INTERNATIONAL SPACE STATION

People can stay in space for months or years at
a time by living on orbiting space stations.

In the 1990s, Russia, the USA, and more than a dozen other countries
came together to build the ISS, the International Space Station.

## QUICK FACTS

Space stations are usually made up of several **MODULES**
that are sent into orbit one at a time, and then
assembled once in space.

The first modules of the ISS were launched in **1998**, and
the station has been in use ever since.

The ISS could fly to the Moon and back in a day.
It reaches speeds of **4.791 MILES PER SECOND**!

The world's **FIRST** space station was the Salyut 1,
launched by the Soviet Union in 1971.

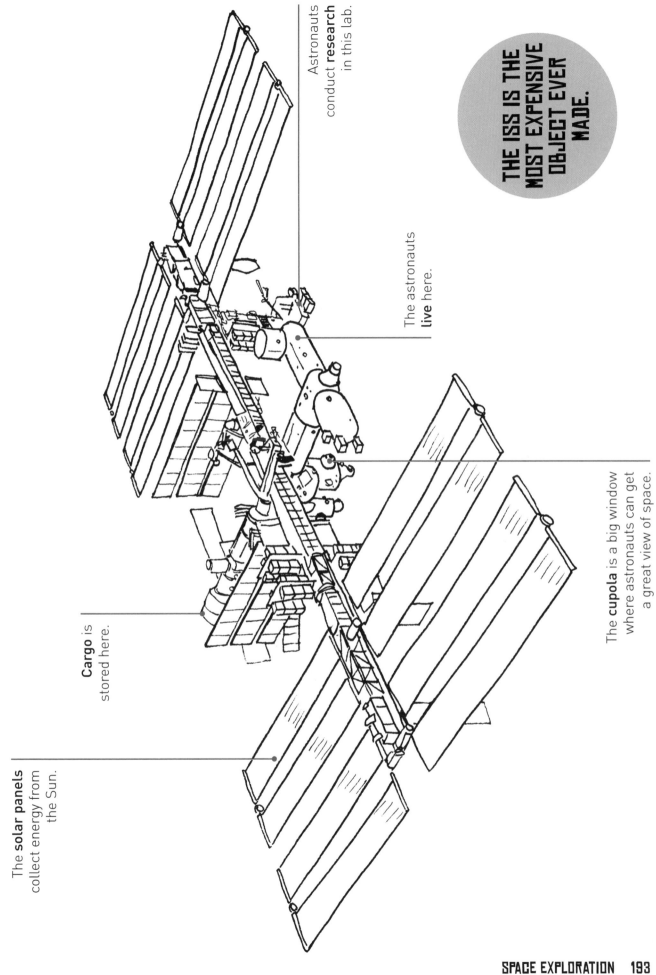

Astronauts conduct **research** in this lab.

THE ISS IS THE MOST EXPENSIVE OBJECT EVER MADE.

The astronauts **live** here.

The **cupola** is a big window where astronauts can get a great view of space.

**Cargo** is stored here.

The **solar panels** collect energy from the Sun.

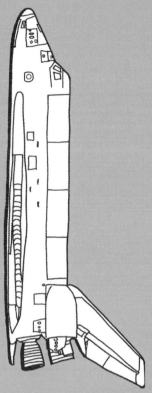

# THE SPACE SHUTTLE

The Americans launched the first space shuttle in 1981. It was developed to provide a reusable, and therefore cheaper, vehicle for launching satellites and for other work in space.

## QUICK FACTS

The space shuttle **PROGRAM** ran from 1981–2011.

At take-off the space shuttle weighed 2,200 tons. It burned almost all of its **FUEL** in the first few minutes after launch.

When it is in **ORBIT** the shuttle's cargo bay opened to release satellites or allow the crew to work in space.

The shuttle landed on a **RUNWAY** just like a conventional aeroplane.

Space agencies are trying different forms of fuel for spacecraft, such as nuclear power, ion drives, or even sailing on the **SOLAR WIND**.

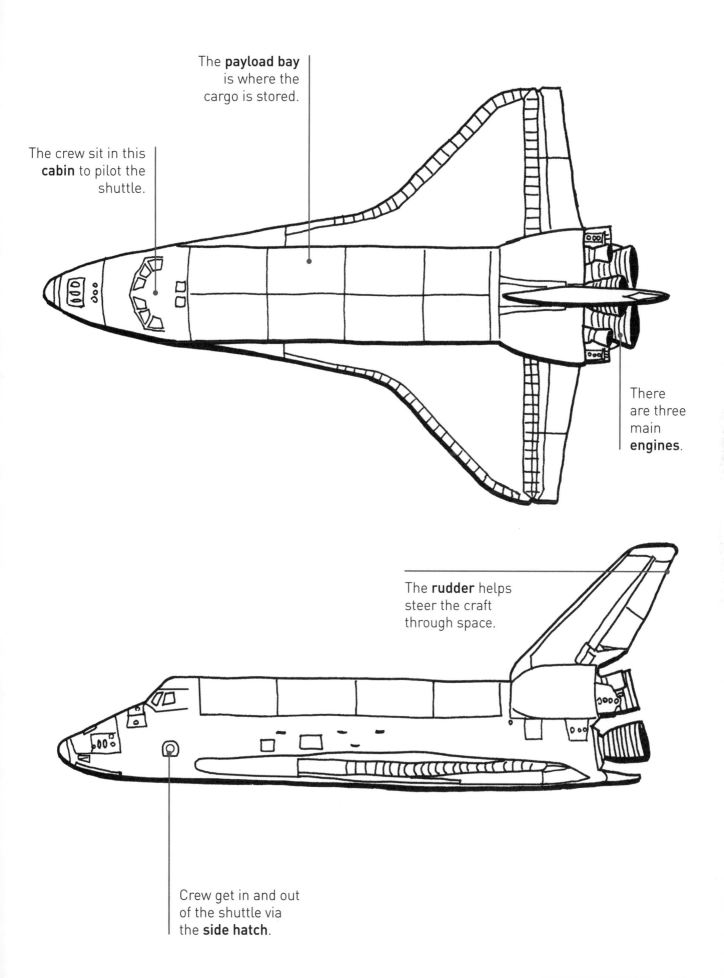

The **payload bay** is where the cargo is stored.

The crew sit in this **cabin** to pilot the shuttle.

There are three main **engines**.

The **rudder** helps steer the craft through space.

Crew get in and out of the shuttle via the **side hatch**.

# ASTRONAUT TRAINING

Candidates for manned spaceflight are carefully screened
to meet the highest physical and mental standards,
and they undergo rigorous training.

Using trainers and mock-ups of actual spacecraft, astronauts
rehearse every exercise from lift-off to recovery, and prepare
for every conceivable malfunction and difficulty.

## QUICK FACTS

In addition to flight training, astronauts are required to have
thorough knowledge of all aspects of space **SCIENCE**, such
as celestial mechanics and rocketry.

NASA has sophisticated **SIMULATORS** that can
reproduce any aspect of a mission on a craft
such as the Space Shuttle.

**PILOTS** can spend time learning how to maneuver the
craft while others can learn how to operate the other
instruments.

NASA astronauts train in a variety of places, including
high-flying **AIRCRAFT**, to learn how to cope with
weightlessness, and in **WATER TANKS**, to learn how
to move in their bulky spacesuits.

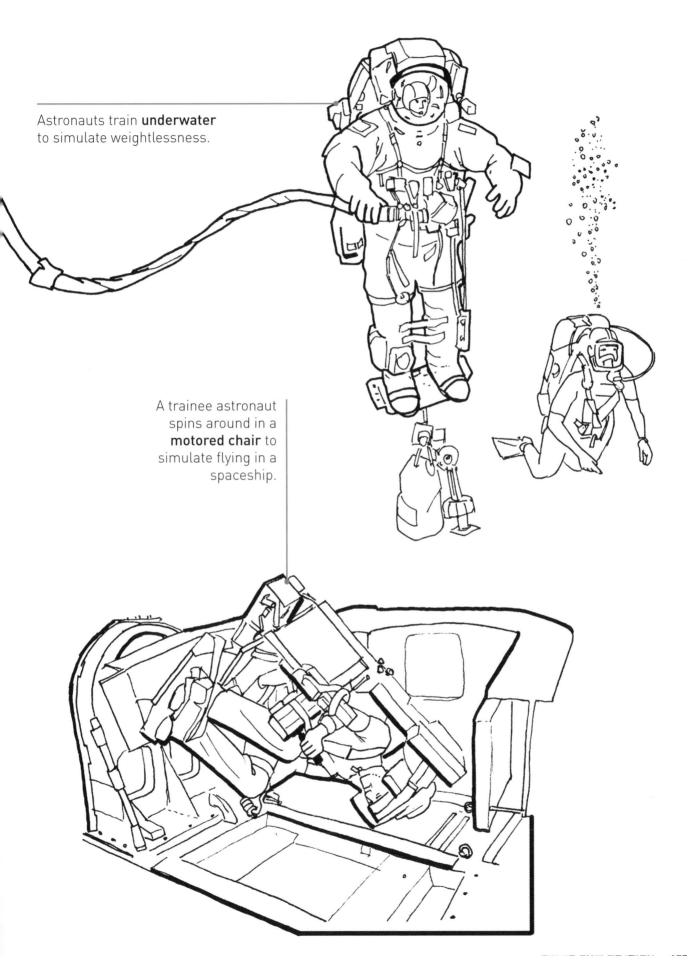

Astronauts train **underwater** to simulate weightlessness.

A trainee astronaut spins around in a **motored chair** to simulate flying in a spaceship.

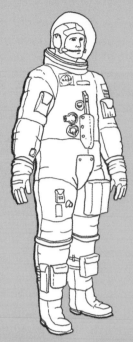

# SURVIVAL IN SPACE

Designing a spacesuit is a very complex procedure, as the spacesuit needs to give the astronaut complete control and protection; in fact, it needs to act like a miniature spacecraft. It provides everything that an astronaut requires to survive for short periods in space.

## QUICK FACTS

Early astronauts found **EATING** in space fairly easy, but the menu consisted of bite-sized cubes, freeze-dried powders, and semi-liquids stuffed in metal tubes.

Muscles do not have to fight against **GRAVITY** in space, so they can waste away. Astronauts must exercise every day.

Astronauts have to **STRAP** themselves to the walls of space stations to stop themselves from floating away.

The lack of gravity causes about a third of people to get **SPACE SICK**.

**BATTERY-POWERED** tools were invented for use in space, where there are no electrical sockets, and the digital watch was invented to help astronauts keep accurate time.

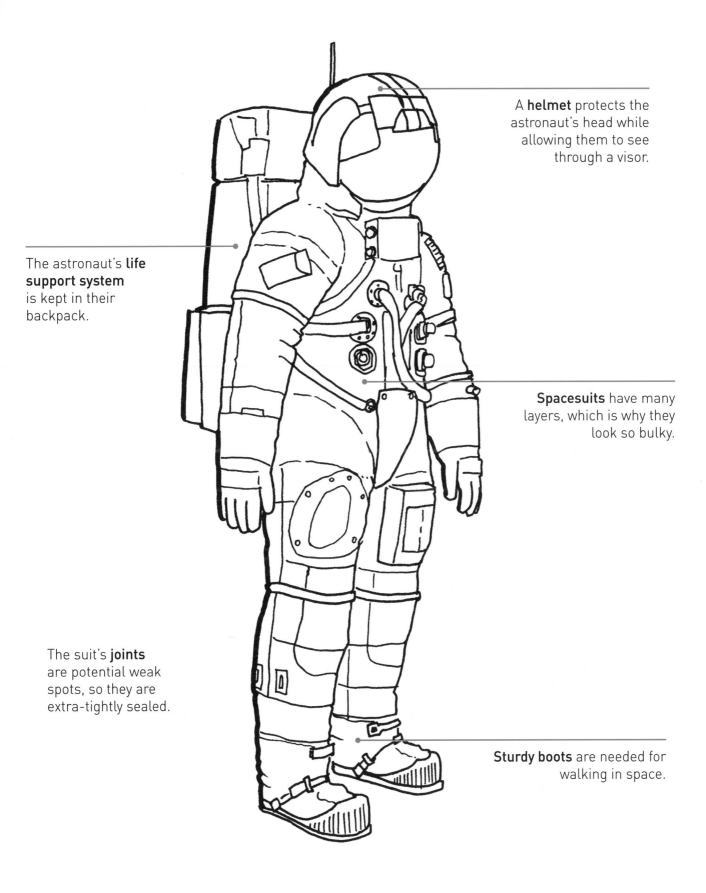

A **helmet** protects the astronaut's head while allowing them to see through a visor.

The astronaut's **life support system** is kept in their backpack.

**Spacesuits** have many layers, which is why they look so bulky.

The suit's **joints** are potential weak spots, so they are extra-tightly sealed.

**Sturdy boots** are needed for walking in space.

# OUTSIDE THE SOLAR SYSTEM

# WHAT IS A STAR?

Stars are huge balls of burning gas that are scattered throughout the Universe.

A new star is born when gas and dust are drawn together by gravity, forming a huge clump. It heats up until a process called nuclear fusion begins, and the new star appears in the sky.

## QUICK FACTS

It takes a few million years for a star to **FORM**, and they last for many millions of years.

The **CLOSEST** stars to Earth are Proxima Centauri and Alpha Centauri.

The distances between stars are so great that a unit for measuring them was worked out, and this is called the **LIGHT-YEAR**. A light-year is the distance that light travels in one year—about 5.88 billion miles!

The **FARTHEST** stars in our galaxy are 80,000 light-years away from us.

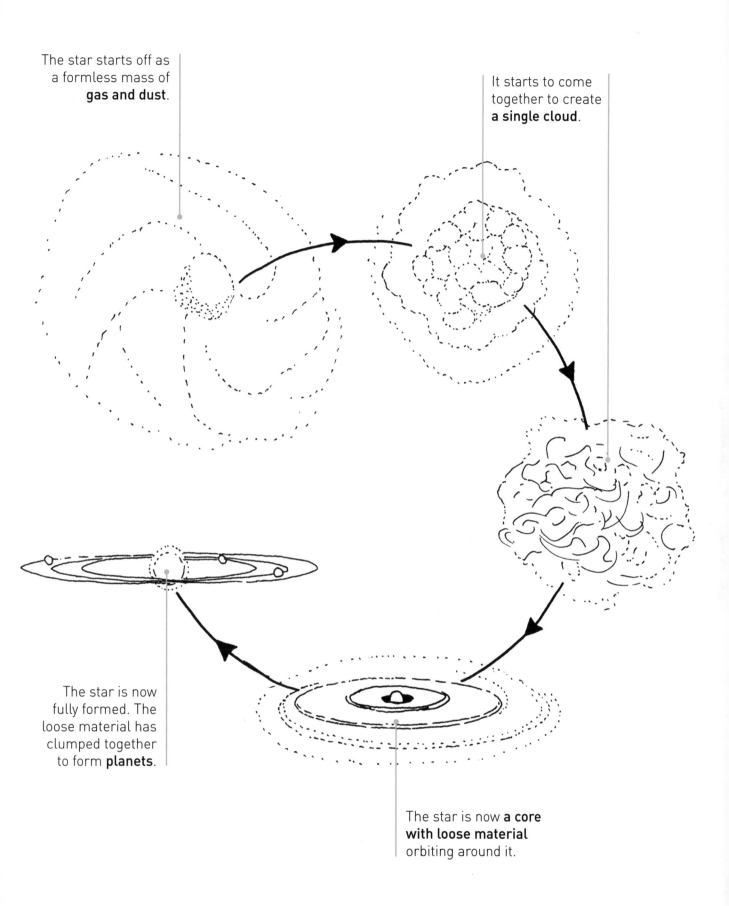

The star starts off as a formless mass of **gas and dust**.

It starts to come together to create **a single cloud**.

The star is now fully formed. The loose material has clumped together to form **planets**.

The star is now **a core with loose material** orbiting around it.

# TYPES OF STARS

Compared to our Sun, some stars are giants.

Our Sun is of a type known as a yellow dwarf. The color of a star shows its surface temperature: red stars are relatively cool, while blue ones are hotter.

The temperatures on their surface range from 6,300°F for cooler stars to over 72,000°F for the hottest stars.

## QUICK FACTS

Many **HUGE** stars contain enough matter to make tens or hundreds of Suns.

The most **COMMON** stars are the same size as the Sun.

Toward the end of its life, a star starts to run out of fuel. It cools, becoming a **RED GIANT**.

Stars die when they eventually use up all their **FUEL** and burn out.

Some stars are not single like the Sun. They have at least one **COMPANION**, and the two orbit each other.

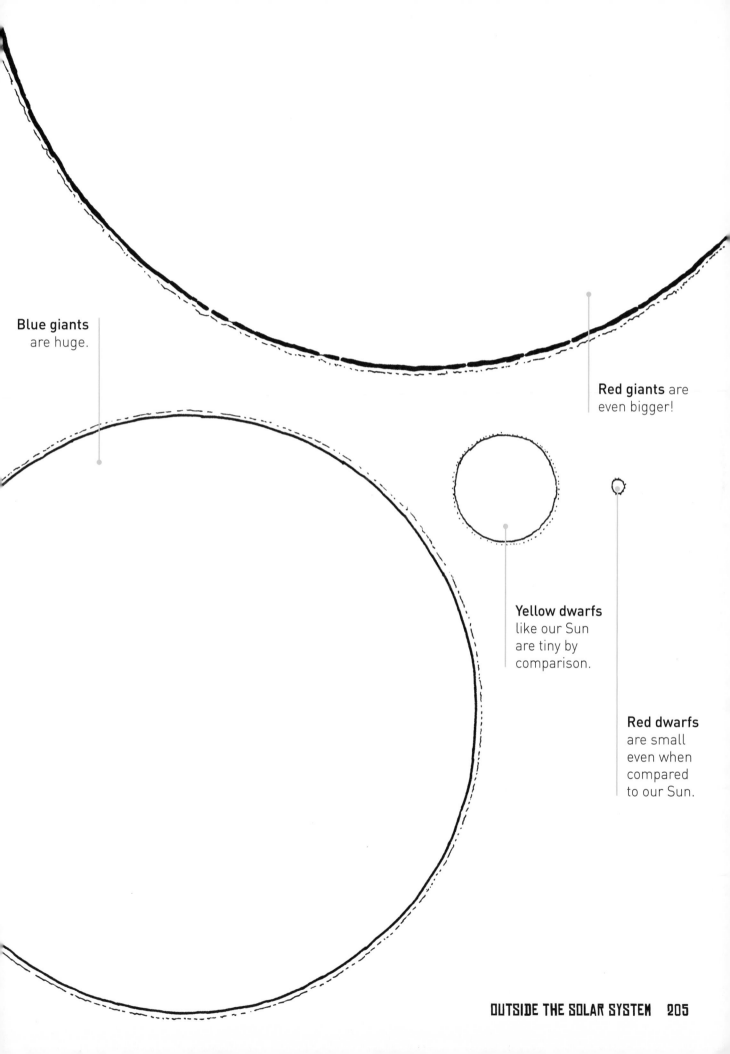

**Blue giants** are huge.

**Red giants** are even bigger!

**Yellow dwarfs** like our Sun are tiny by comparison.

**Red dwarfs** are small even when compared to our Sun.

# WATCHING THE SKIES

Of all the stars in the sky, you can only see about 6,000
without a telescope. The most you would be able to count
at any one time would be a little over 1,000 stars.

## QUICK FACTS

In the night sky, all stars appear to be the **SAME** size.

A star's **BRIGHTNESS** depends on how bright it really is,
its size, how hot it is, and how far away.

Most stars burn **STEADILY**, and if we could see them
from space, they would not actually be twinkling at all.

The appeance of **TWINKLING** is caused by the light
passing through Earth's atmosphere—it is bent by
changes in the air temperature.

Sometimes a giant star explodes and is blown to pieces.
This is called a **SUPERNOVA**.

You can see the brightest stars with the **naked eye**.

With a **telescope** you can see many more thousands of stars.

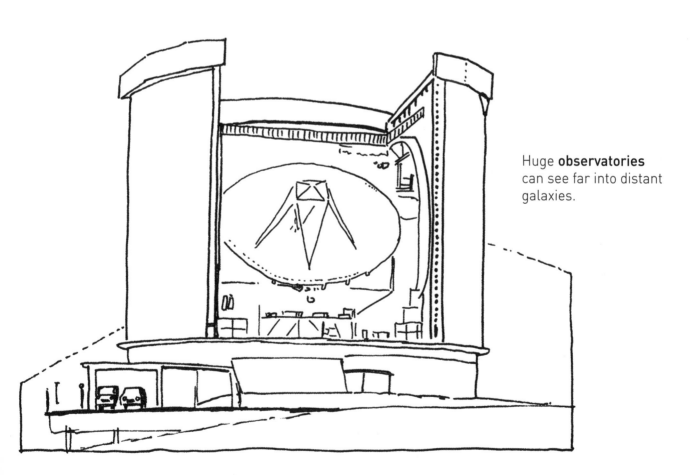

Huge **observatories** can see far into distant galaxies.

# CONSTELLATIONS

People have seen patterns in the stars since ancient times. The groups of stars that form these patterns are called constellations.

However, the stars in a constellation rarely have any connection with one another. They simply lie in the same direction when viewed from Earth.

Twelve of the most ancient constellations have special significance. They are the constellations that the Sun, Moon, and planets pass through. They are known as the Signs of the Zodiac.

## QUICK FACTS

There are a total of **88** constellations.

The **NAMES** in use today have been handed down to us from the Romans and Greeks.

Most constellations were named according to religious beliefs and **MYTHOLOGICAL** characters.

The **OLDEST** constellations were probably named more than 4,000 years ago.

In 1930, the International Astronomical Union **MAPPED** the boundaries between constellations, so that there were no gaps. Every star now belongs to a constellation.

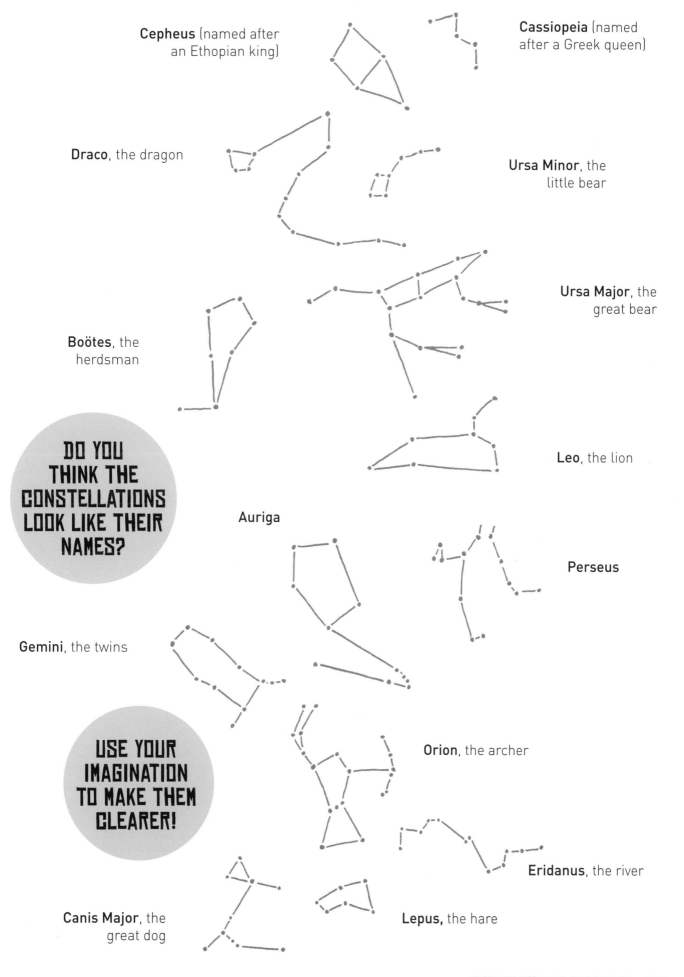

Cepheus (named after an Ethopian king)

Cassiopeia (named after a Greek queen)

Draco, the dragon

Ursa Minor, the little bear

Ursa Major, the great bear

Boötes, the herdsman

Leo, the lion

**DO YOU THINK THE CONSTELLATIONS LOOK LIKE THEIR NAMES?**

Auriga

Perseus

Gemini, the twins

**USE YOUR IMAGINATION TO MAKE THEM CLEARER!**

Orion, the archer

Eridanus, the river

Canis Major, the great dog

Lepus, the hare

# THE MILKY WAY

Our star, the Sun, is one of billions of stars that travel through space together. This vast collection of stars is called the Milky Way galaxy.

On a clear dark night, you may be able to see the hazy band of the Milky Way stretching across the sky. The stars are held together by the pull of their gravity.

## QUICK FACTS

--------------------------------------------------

The Milky Way is a thin **DISC** of stars with a thicker bulge in the middle. It is sometimes described as looking like two fried eggs back to back!

--------------------------------------------------

The disc is surrounded by a ball-shaped "**HALO**" of clusters containing very old stars. The Milky Way may once have been ball-shaped before it became a disc.

--------------------------------------------------

There are at least **300 BILLION** stars in the Milky Way.

--------------------------------------------------

In early Christian times people thought the Milky Way was a pathway for **ANGELS** to travel to Heaven.

--------------------------------------------------

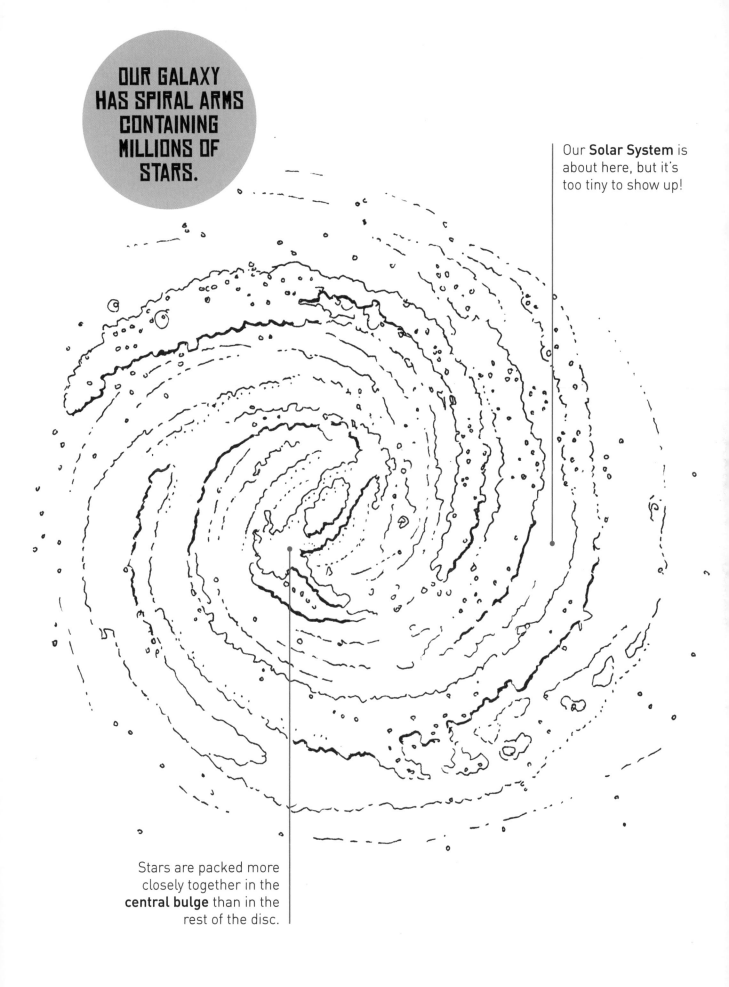

**OUR GALAXY HAS SPIRAL ARMS CONTAINING MILLIONS OF STARS.**

Our **Solar System** is about here, but it's too tiny to show up!

Stars are packed more closely together in the **central bulge** than in the rest of the disc.

# OTHER GALAXIES

There are billions of giant star groups like the Milky Way. They are called galaxies.

Our galaxy, the Milky Way, belongs to a cluster of about 30 galaxies called the Local Group. This is one of about 400 clusters of galaxies that form a grouping called the Local Supercluster.

## QUICK FACTS

There could be as many as **100 BILLION** galaxies in the universe.

All galaxies have one of three basic **SHAPES**—spiral, elliptical, or irregular. This classification was devised by American astronomer Edwin Hubble in the 1920s.

Nearly all **GALAXIES** are spiral or elliptical in shape.

Many of them are grouped together in **CLUSTERS** with huge areas of space between them, and consequently form many irregular shapes.

**SPIRAL** galaxies are usually made up of young stars.

Irregular galaxy

Elliptical galaxy

Barred spiral galaxy

Spiral galaxy

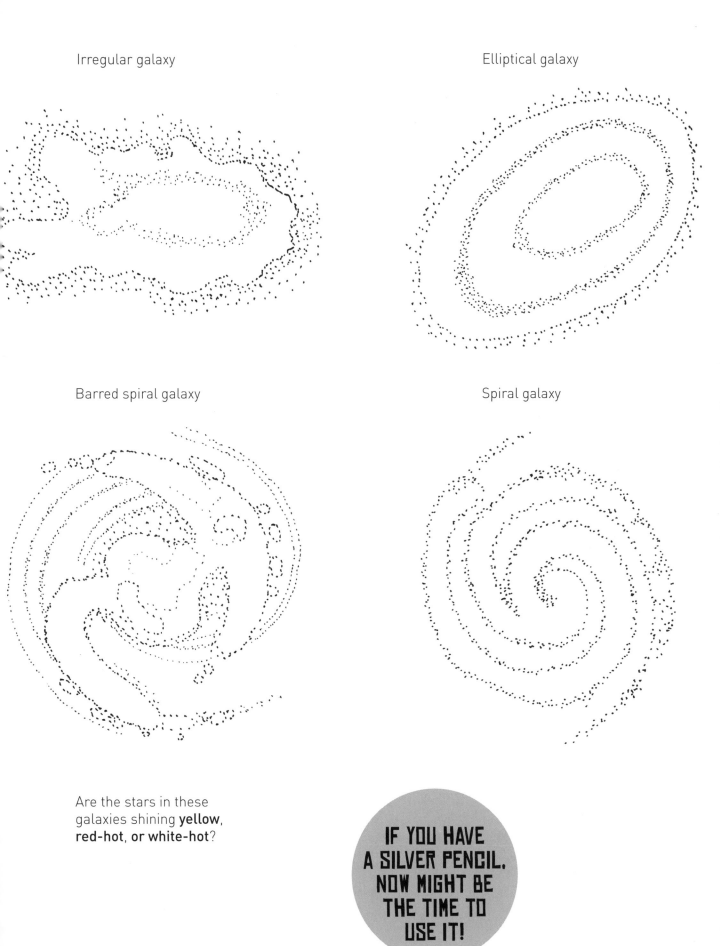

Are the stars in these galaxies shining **yellow**, **red-hot, or white-hot**?

IF YOU HAVE A SILVER PENCIL, NOW MIGHT BE THE TIME TO USE IT!

# NEBULAE

A nebula is a huge cloud of white-hot gas and solid material that whirls about in interstellar space getting smaller and hotter all the time. As the gas cloud grows smaller, it throws off rings of gas. Each of these rings condenses to become a star.

## QUICK FACTS

A nebula looks **SOLID**. However, it is mostly composed of dust and gas which slowly condenses into stars.

The Orion nebula is visible with the naked eye. Stars are being **BORN** there right now.

**DARK** nebulae appear as irregularly shaped black patches and blot out the light of the stars beyond them.

**BRIGHT** nebulae appear as faintly luminous, glowing surfaces. They either emit their own light or reflect the light of nearby stars.

There are many **THOUSANDS** of nebulae in our galaxy.

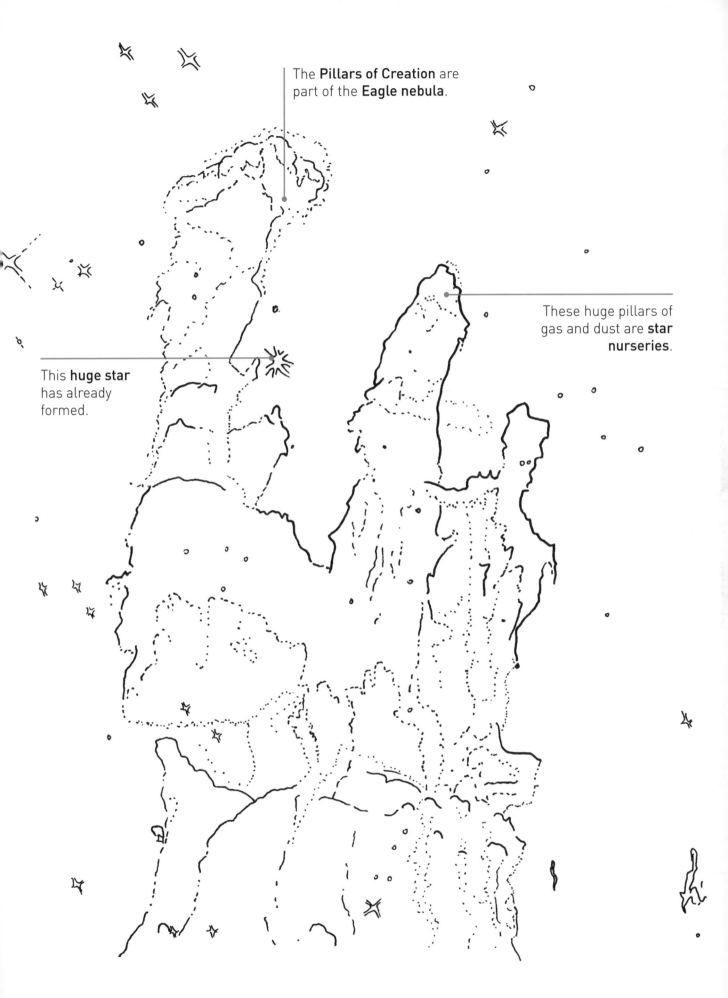

The **Pillars of Creation** are part of the **Eagle nebula**.

These huge pillars of gas and dust are **star nurseries**.

This **huge star** has already formed.

# SUPERNOVAS AND BLACK HOLES

A supernova happens when a star collapses as it begins to burn out, then suddenly explodes, producing a huge amount of light.

This leaves behind a tiny core of neutrons: the heaviest substance in the Universe. The gravity of this material is so powerful that it pulls in everything around it.

## QUICK FACTS

The **MILKY WAY** only has around two supernovae per century, and they are very difficult to spot.

The light given off by a supernova can be brighter than the light given off by an **ENTIRE GALAXY**.

Black holes are the **DARKEST** objects in space.

Even **LIGHT** itself is sucked into a black hole. Nothing that goes in ever comes out.

We cannot **SEE** black holes. We can identify them from the radio waves given off as a star is drawn into one.

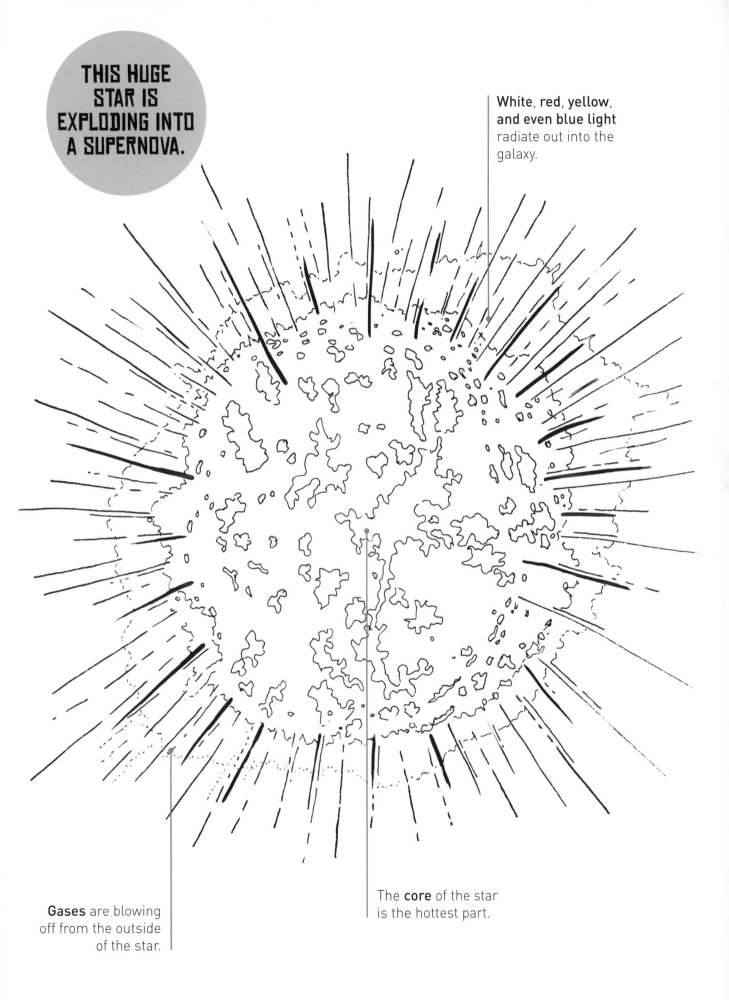

THIS HUGE STAR IS EXPLODING INTO A SUPERNOVA.

White, red, yellow, and even blue light radiate out into the galaxy.

Gases are blowing off from the outside of the star.

The core of the star is the hottest part.

# THE UNIVERSE

The Universe is all the matter, energy, space, and time that exists everywhere. Scientists have tried many theories to explain how and when the Universe began.

Today, most scientists agree that the Universe burst into existence about 13.7 billion years ago in a huge explosion called the Big Bang. It flung matter and energy in all directions and produced the Universe we know today.

## QUICK FACTS

Scientists who study the origin and development of the Universe are called **COSMOLOGISTS**.

Nobody knows what **SHAPE** the universe is.

The Universe is **MADE UP** almost entirely of hydrogen and helium. All other kinds of matter are very rare.

**BEFORE** the Big Bang, everything in the Universe was packed into an area smaller than an atom.

Most astronomers believe that the universe we see is only **PART** of the whole universe.

How far does it really extend, and does it go on forever? **NOBODY KNOWS**.

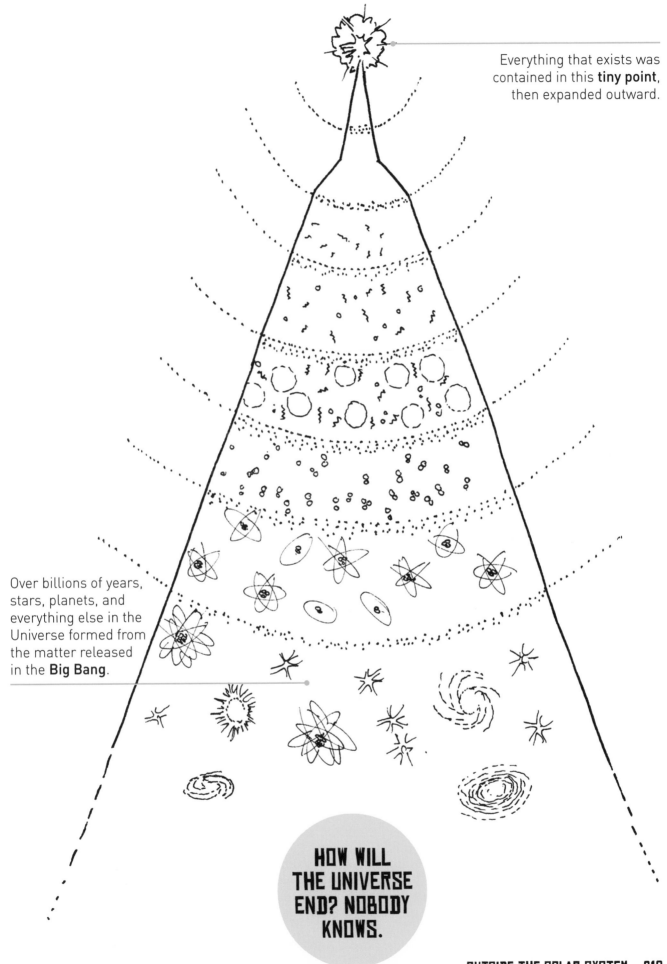

Everything that exists was contained in this **tiny point**, then expanded outward.

Over billions of years, stars, planets, and everything else in the Universe formed from the matter released in the **Big Bang**.

HOW WILL THE UNIVERSE END? NOBODY KNOWS.

# IS THERE ALIEN LIFE?

As far as we know, there is no form of life on any
of the other planets in the Solar System.

Hower, there are some life-forms on Earth that need neither light
nor oxygen as they live in a system that depends on sulphur from
deep undersea volcanoes in conditions of extreme heat and pressure.

So some scientists hope that life-forms might exist in similar
extreme conditions elsewhere in the Solar System.

## QUICK FACTS

Scientists consider Saturn's moon Titan and Jupiter's moon
Europa to be the most **LIKELY** places for life to be found.

In 1996, a NASA team reported that they had found evidence
of microscopic **LIFE ON MARS**. The tiny microbes were found
inside a meteorite which had traveled from Mars to Earth.
However, many scientists disagree with their findings.

A light or object in the air that has no obvious explanation
is called an "unidentified flying object", or **UFO**.

Many reported UFOs are **ACTUALLY** planets, stars,
or meteors.

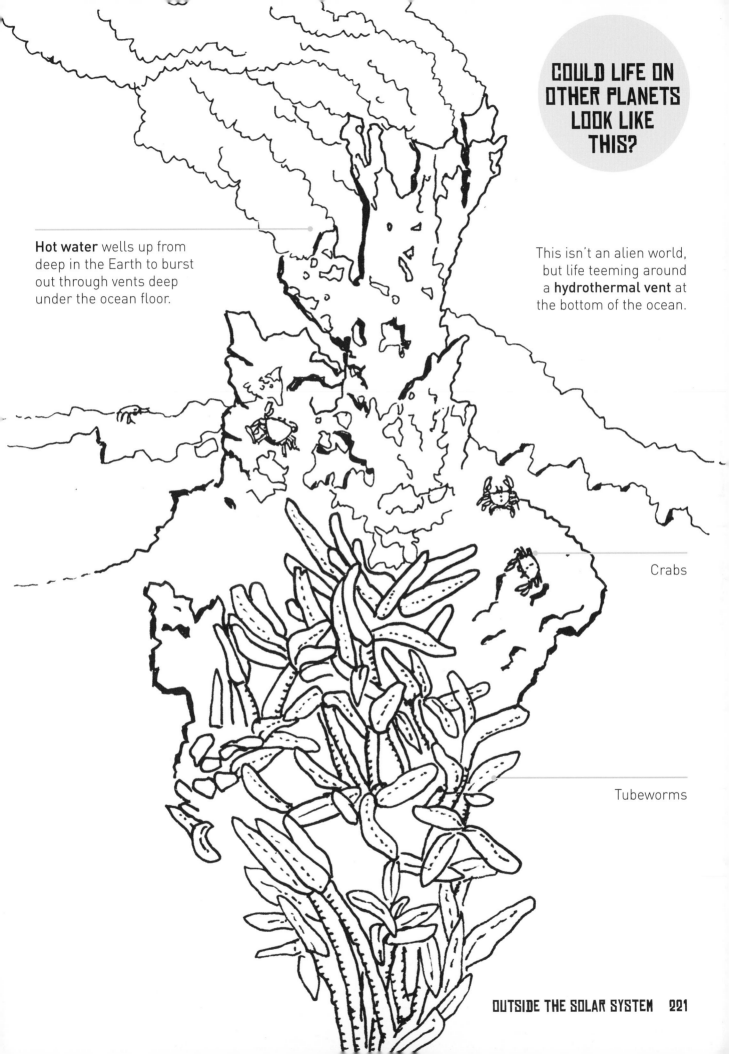

**Hot water** wells up from deep in the Earth to burst out through vents deep under the ocean floor.

This isn't an alien world, but life teeming around a **hydrothermal vent** at the bottom of the ocean.

Crabs

Tubeworms

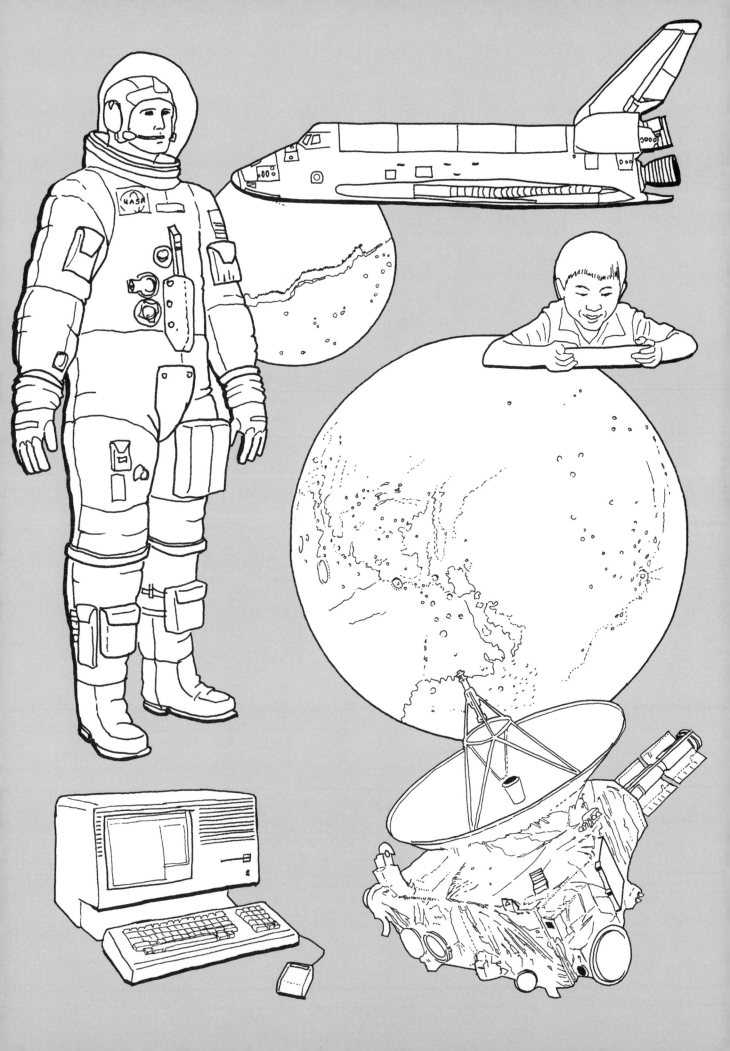

# Look out for all three of the fantastic Color + Learn titles:

*Prehistoric World*
*Human Body*
*Science and Space*

These amazing books all have more than
200 pages of facts and coloring fun!